CAMBRIDGE LIBRARY COLLECTION

Books of enduring scholarly value

History

The books reissued in this series include accounts of historical events and movements by eye-witnesses and contemporaries, as well as landmark studies that assembled significant source materials or developed new historiographical methods. The series includes work in social, political and military history on a wide range of periods and regions, giving modern scholars ready access to influential publications of the past.

A Narrative of the Battle of St. Vincent

Lieutenant-Colonel John Drinkwater (1762–1844), an army officer, was on board the *Minerva*, bearing Commodore Nelson's pennant, after the British evacuation from Corsica, when they found themselves in the middle of the Spanish fleet. Having been transferred to another ship, and Nelson to the *Captain*, Drinkwater thus became an eyewitness of the Battle of St Vincent, 14 February 1797. He made sketches of the positions of the fleet during the battle that were subsequently praised for their accuracy by naval officers. His *Narrative* was originally published the same year, but reissued in 1840 with the addition of anecdotes of Nelson, to raise funds for a Nelson testimonial. The original aim of the work was to give due credit to the officers, particularly Nelson, to whom it was felt that Admiral Sir John Jervis had not given sufficient recognition for their part in his most significant victory.

CAMBRIDGE UNIVERSITY PRESS

Cambridge, New York, Melbourne, Madrid, Cape Town, Singapore,
São Paolo, Delhi, Dubai, Tokyo, Mexico City

Published in the United States of America by Cambridge University Press, New York

www.cambridge.org
Information on this title: www.cambridge.org/9781108024372

© in this compilation Cambridge University Press 2010

This edition first published 1840
This digitally printed version 2010

ISBN 978-1-108-02437-2 Paperback

Horatio Nelson
1797

Commanding
H. M. SHIP CAPTAIN
of 74 Guns
IN THE BATTLE of ST VINCENT
14th February
1797.

Drawn by H. Corbould

Engraved by Scriven & Misan

Published by Saunders & Otley Conduit Street.

A NARRATIVE

OF THE

BATTLE OF ST. VINCENT;

WITH

ANECDOTES

OF

NELSON,

BEFORE AND AFTER THAT BATTLE.

BY

COLONEL DRINKWATER BETHUNE, F.S.A.,

AUTHOR OF THE "HISTORY OF THE SIEGE OF GIBRALTAR," ETC.

SECOND EDITION.

Palmam qui meruit ferat.

LONDON:

SAUNDERS AND OTLEY, CONDUIT STREET.

MDCCCXL.

PRINTED BY WILLIAM WILCOCKSON, ROLLS BUILDINGS, FETTER LANE.

TO

SIR GEORGE COCKBURN, G. C. B.,

&c. &c. &c.

My Dear Sir George,

Having decided to publish a Second Edition of my " Narrative of the Proceedings of the British Fleet, commanded by Admiral Sir John Jervis, K.B., in the action with the Spanish Fleet off Cape St. Vincent, on the 14th of February, 1797," with additional anecdotes of Nelson, I am induced to request that you will allow this publication to be inscribed with your name ; not only as the associate and intimate friend of the gallant Nelson, whose transcendant conduct in that glorious battle, the publication of the original " Narrative" was in-tended to commemorate, but as one of the only three Commanders now surviving, who were present on that occasion. In addition to these reasons, I

gladly embrace this public opportunity of expressing
my high estimation of your eminent professional
talents, and of manifesting my sincere and grateful
recollection of many acts of friendship and kindness
received at your hands.

With sentiments of warm attachment and regard,

Believe me to be,

My dear Sir George,

Yours most sincerely,

J. Drinkwater Bethune.

Thorncroft,
Surrey,
14th February, 1840.

PREFACE.

———

THE first edition of the " Narrative of the Battle of St. Vincent" was published in the spring of 1797, but, being anonymous, did not obtain the full credit to which it was entitled; and one of the main objects of the present edition, is to establish the authenticity of that narrative, and to explain the circumstances which led to its publication.

It had been the good fortune of the Author to witness that celebrated battle. Being previously acquainted with many of the principal officers serving in the action, he felt more than a common interest in their personal welfare. Never were British seamanship and valour more eminently exemplified than on that occasion. Nothing was wanting to render the transactions of that splendid

day complete, but a satisfactory record of the
various occurrences, such as would afford not only
a description of the engagement, but due notice
of the personal conduct of those individuals to
whose extraordinary bravery and skill the discom-
fiture of a greatly superior force was to be attributed. The Admiral's public letter was, however,
little calculated to gratify the legitimate anxiety
of the nation on this subject. Instead of detailing
the movements of the British fleet in an action that
reflected the highest honor on Sir John Jervis himself, as well as on his gallant squadron, and properly
noticing the distinguished conduct and bearing of
the commanders of his Majesty's ships Culloden,
Blenheim, and particularly of the Captain, (in which
ship the chivalrous and daring Nelson carried his
commodore's pendant,) the Admiral's public despatches were limited to an official report of his
meeting with the Spanish fleet off Cape St. Vincent,
a brief and meagre description of the manœuvres of
the British squadron during the action, and of the
enemy's defeat with the loss of four sail of the line.
Not even the slightest mention was made of any of
the gallant officers who had so ably seconded their

Chief in obtaining that victory. The conduct of Commodore Nelson had been pre-eminently distinguished: two of the four captured ships were taken solely by him. The whole of the British squadron had not hesitated to bestow on him the chief merit of the enemy's defeat; therefore, not to have his name even mentioned in the official public despatch, (usually considered the proper channel for recording extraordinary exertions on such occasions, and too often, the only gratification afforded to the parties named,) produced no small degree of surprise among the Commodore's personal friends. Some of these had been witnesses of his undaunted conduct in the action, and of its results; and they were greatly at a loss to conceive any plausible reasons for concealing such acts of heroism from the public.

No sooner was the Admiral's letter published, than Nelson's friends were not backward in expressing their disappointment at its silence with respect to the heroes of St. Valentine's day—a silence that appeared to them a real injustice to all parties. They called for a publication of particulars, and it was not long before an attempt was made to gratify their reasonable expectations.

It was known that the Author had sketched a
series of diagrams of the position of the fleets
during the battle. These diagrams had been corrected on the spot, by communication with many of
the principal actors, and being generally admitted
to exhibit a tolerably correct view of the battle at
different periods of the action, it had been intended
to lay them before the public. The Author was
now strongly urged to accompany their appearance
with a description of the battle, which it was also
well known he had likewise drawn up for the
gratification of a private circle. Concurring with
the friends of Nelson in the expediency of some
such publication, the Author was persuaded to
comply with their wishes, by annexing the private
letter to the diagrams. Hence the original Narrative of the Battle. To answer the object in view
by its publication, its early appearance became of
moment, and it was given to the public without
alteration. No name was affixed to the pamphlet,
the author wishing thereby to mark his sense of the
presumption of an officer of His Majesty's land
forces, in attempting the description of a naval
engagement. It was afterwards thought that this

scruple needed not to have been so strongly felt, and indeed, it proved unfavorable to the Author's main object; since the fact that the Narrative was published anonymously, threw a doubt on its authenticity, and the pamphlet consequently had but a very limited sale. Indeed, it did not attract any special public notice until its accuracy was promulgated by the officers of Sir John Jervis's fleet, and particularly through the testimony of Nelson himself,* too late, however, to repay even the expence of the publication ; for by the time the accuracy of the account became established, the greatest part of the impression had been consigned to the usual fate of unsaleable articles. The writer was, however, most amply rewarded by the increased friendship of the gallant Commodore, who, from that moment, never omitted any opportunity of acknowledging to him his personal obligation, particularly on a

* See Clarke and M'Arthur's Life of Nelson, page 51. Extract from Lord Nelson's Summary of his professional career, drawn up by himself:—

" For an account of what passed from our sailing from Porto Ferrajo, on the 29th of January, 1797, to the finish of the action on the 14th of February, I refer to the Narrative published by Colonel Drinkwater. '

memorable occasion which the Author cannot deny
himself the gratification of recording here. The
first time that he met Lord Nelson after the Battle
of the Nile, the Admiral approached, with the
eagerness which always characterised him, and
shaking the Author cordially by the hand, exclaimed, "Why were not you with us at Aboukir?"

It was afterwards understood that Sir John Jervis
wrote two public letters descriptive of the battle of
the 14th of February; in the first of which the
Admiral, impressed with a due sense of the merits
of his officers, gave appropriate credit to those of
superior rank, and high praise to Nelson and others
for their distinguished conduct on that occasion;
but that the first letter was suppressed, and a second
substituted in its place, on his being reminded of
the inconveniences that had been found to result,
on other occasions, from the practice of naming
officers in public despatches.*

---

* Extract from Sir John Barrow's Life of Admiral Lord Howe,
published in 1838-9 :—

"He (Lord Howe) would have acted, if left to his own judgment, as
Sir John Jervis did, after the battle of St. Vincent, who omitted even the
name of Nelson, though he was mainly instrumental in gaining the battle. It is known, however, that in Jervis's original letter, he had given to

Sir John Jervis, in addition to his public letter, likewise wrote a private one to the First Lord of the Admiralty; but in that private communication, the Admiral entered into very few details; nor did it speak of Nelson as his conduct, in the opinion of those who witnessed it, certainly merited. All that was said of his heroic achievements was, "that Commodore Nelson contributed much to the fortune of the day."

The first edition of "the Narrative" is now rarely to be met with, and the Author has been frequently urged to republish it. Hitherto, he has resisted these representations; but, as the public attention appears again to be awakened to the merits of the Hero of Trafalgar, by the recently declared intention to erect a suitable testimonial to

Nelson all due praise; but was prevailed on by Sir Robert Calder, the Captain of the fleet, to substitute another, in which it was left out, on the ground that as Nelson had disobeyed the signal of recall, any eulogy on his conduct would encourage other officers to do the same, while the exclusive praise of one individual would act as a discouragement of the rest."

The writer of Lord Howe's Life adds, very pointedly and properly, "The surprise is, that a man of Lord St. Vincent's sagacity should not have detected the lurking jealousy that gave rise to such a recommendation."

perpetuate the memory of his invaluable public services, the present moment appeared favorable for that purpose. For these reasons, and with the view of adding any profits which may accrue from the sale to the sum already contributed to the fund for erecting a memorial to do honor to the immortal Nelson, the Author has decided to republish " The Narrative of the Battle of St. Vincent." Some interesting anecdotes, with other additional matter not deemed necessary to notice in the first hasty edition, are likewise introduced, affording, on the whole, new and corroborative proofs, if such were wanting, of the high professional feeling and zeal, uncommon sagacity, and prompt decision which were united in Nelson, even on minor occasions, with a degree of personal activity and energy that was almost without a parallel.

NARRATIVE

OF THE

BATTLE OF ST. VINCENT,

&c. &c. &c.

FROM the statements already given in the Preface, it will be evident that the main object in publishing the original Narrative of the Battle of St. Vincent, was to do honor to Commodore Nelson, who had borne so pre-eminent a share in that celebrated action.

In re-publishing that work, and adding such new matter as it is now intended to do, in the view of increasing its interest, the object is equally to extend, if possible, that gallant hero's renown. To make these additions more intelligible, I shall be obliged to go back to an earlier date, from which I shall give a brief sketch of some public transactions with which Commodore Nelson was connected previous to the 14th of February, 1797.

Admiral Lord Hood arrived in the Mediterranean at the commencement of the French revolutionary war, in the summer of 1793. The plan of this publication does not lead me to do more than cursorily allude to his Lordship's splendid service in obtaining possession of the French arsenal of Toulon—to the interesting defence of that important fortress against the French republicans—the withdrawal of Lord Hood, with the combined forces, from Toulon, and his Lordship's subsequent occupation of Corsica. Nelson at that time commanded the Agamemnon, of sixty-four guns, which formed a part of Lord Hood's fleet. In this ship he was most actively employed, and was charged, amongst other duties, to watch the French garrisons in Corsica, and ultimately, he acted, as is well known, a very distinguished part in the subsequent sieges of the cities of Bastia and Calvi by the British forces. When Corsica became an appendage of the British crown, Nelson was employed in many transactions connected with that island, and thereby ample opportunities were afforded to him of becoming intimately acquainted with Sir Gilbert Elliot, the Viceroy, and with most of the public functionaries acting under his Excellency's government; in which number I had the good fortune to be included.

When the measure for evacuating Corsica was decided upon, and the arrangements were made for withdrawing the troops and stores, Nelson had the special charge of superintending the retirement of the Viceroy from Bastia, the seat of government; likewise, the embarkation of the stores and troops of that garrison. It is almost needless to add that he executed this service, which was of no small difficulty, in a manner that marked decision and firmness, as well as superior talents and professional skill. About this time he had been removed from the Agamemnon to the command of the Captain, of seventy-four guns, and promoted to carry a broad pendant.

On giving up Corsica, the Viceroy had determined to occupy Porto Ferrajo, in the island of Elba, a fortress of considerable strength, where the British army might remain until Government were made acquainted with the position of public affairs in the northern parts of Italy : Commodore Nelson escorted the Viceroy and troops from Bastia to Elba.

When Lord Hood resigned the command of the Mediterranean fleet, he was succeeded by Admiral Hotham, who again, in a short time, was succeeded by Admiral Sir John Jervis.

At the period when the British fleet appeared in the Mediterranean in 1793, Spain was acting in

union with England against France; but in 1796
she had made an alliance with the French Republic,
declaring war against Great Britain: and the expected junction of the French and Spanish fleets,
(which afterwards actually took place at Toulon,)
was understood to be one of the chief reasons which
induced the British Cabinet to abandon Corsica,
and to order the British fleet to retire from the
Mediterranean.

The Viceroy had been some weeks in possession
of Elba, and the British Admiral, after collecting
the Levant trade and his distant cruizers, had
sailed for Gibraltar, when it occurred to Sir Gilbert
that the interval, until he received the reply of
Government to his representations respecting the
occupation of Porto Ferrajo, might be profitably
employed in a visit to the Italian States in amity
with Great Britain, to whom he had been, from
an early period, accredited. He therefore availed
himself of the occasion, to repair to Naples, and
subsequently to Rome, and to have a personal communication with those governments regarding the
actual position of their affairs, in consequence of
Buonaparte's active and successful movements in
the north of Italy.

When Sir John Jervis arrived at Gibraltar, he
found fresh orders from England, directing him to

withdraw the British troops from Elba, and orders were immediately given for the execution of this unexpected service, which was entrusted to Nelson. He was ordered to remove his pendant from the Captain of seventy-four guns, to La Minerve, a frigate of thirty-eight guns, commanded by Captain George Cockburn, which ship, with another frigate, the Blanche, of thirty-two guns. commanded by Captain Preston, was placed under Commodore Nelson's orders, for this special service.

On his passage from Gibraltar to Elba, the Commodore, on the night of the 19th of December, fell in with two Spanish frigates, the largest of which carrying a stern light, he brought to action, and after a very spirited engagement of upwards of two hours, captured her; whilst the Blanche was directed to pursue the other frigate, which after a short action submitted. Captain Cockburn, on taking possession of his prize, found her to be the Santa Sabina, of forty guns and 286 men, commanded by Don Jacobo Steuart, whose loss in the action was stated by him to be 164 men killed and wounded. The British officers and men detached to secure the Sabina had scarcely got on board of her, and the Minerve taken her in tow, when the Minerve was assailed by a fresh frigate, which, after cutting off her prize, she soon obliged to sheer off; but, at the same time, Captain Cockburn discovered that three other ships, one of them of the line, were approaching him, and at no great distance. The Minerve was now compelled to consult her own safety, which, by good seamanship and address, crippled as she had been in the late fight, was happily effected, although with the painful sacrifice of two of her lieutenants, Culverhouse and Hardy, who, with a sufficient party, had been sent on board the prize. At the moment, the loss of these officers was an occurrence much regretted by both the Commodore and Captain Cockburn ; but eventually, the circumstance proved of very great importance, and amply repaid them for their temporary mortification. The Blanche had not taken possession of her prize, when she was obliged to abandon her, and was equally fortunate in making her escape. The loss of the Minerve in her two actions, amounted to seven killed and forty-four wounded.

On the 27th of December, Nelson reached Porto Ferrajo. Sir Gilbert Elliot was then absent on his visit to the Italian States, but intelligence of the Commodore's arrival was immediately sent to him. On the return of the Viceroy to Elba, a consultation was held between Sir Gilbert Elliot, Lieutenant-General De Burgh (who commanded the troops,) and Commodore Nelson, respecting the late orders from Government at home, which Nelson had been specially deputed by the Admiral to carry into effect. The subject was one of great difficulty, involving many interests, and had of course the most deliberate consideration, the result of which was that, under existing circumstances, it was deemed of paramount importance that the British troops should, notwithstanding those orders, continue in possession of Elba, until his Majesty's Ministers could be fully apprized of the many cogent reasons for that course of proceeding.

This decision, however, only affected General De Burgh and the troops. The naval stores brought away from Corsica were, in pursuance of Sir John Jervis's orders, to be removed immediately from Porto Ferrajo.

Every exertion was now used in completing the repairs of the Minerve, and executing the other arrangements connected with the Commodore's early return to Sir John Jervis.

It was highly expedient that Sir Gilbert Elliot should see the British Admiral, if possible, and make known to him the general purport of what he had collected on his late visit to the courts of Naples and Rome ; and therefore it was arranged that Sir Gilbert Elliot should embark with Nelson and Captain Cockburn in the Minerve. In this frigate, accompanied by the Romulus, of thirty-six

guns, commanded by Captain George Hope, the
Commodore proposed to reconnoitre, on his way
back, every port of the enemy, French and Spanish,
where it was probable he might collect any intelligence regarding the employment of the enemy's
naval force, and their equipment, &c. Captain
M'Namara, in the Southampton frigate, was destined to take charge of the store and hospital ships,
Dromedary and Dolphin, and the Dido and Sincere
frigates were directed to have under their convoy
the twelve naval transports, and any ships that
chose to avail themselves of their protection. The
two latter divisions had special instructions to take
different courses, in order that they might be less
embarrassed, should they on their passage fall in
with the enemy's fleet—an event then considered
as not very unlikely to occur.

With Sir Gilbert Elliot, were embarked in the
Minerve, Monsieur Pozzo di Borgo, (Secretary of
State in Corsica during its connection with Great
Britain,) who was now seeking a retreat under British protection, and several members of his Excellency's late Corsican establishment. On board of
the Romulus, Mr. Hardman, private secretary to
the Viceroy, and myself, were embarked.

The three divisions left Porto Ferrajo on the
same day, the 29th of January, 1797, and each

pursued a distinct and separate course for its
ultimate destination—viz., the British fleet, at a
rendezvous already indicated by the Admiral, not
very distant from the western entrance of the Straits
of Gibraltar.

Leaving Porto Ferrajo, Commodore Nelson steered
directly for Cape Corse, to look into the Gulf of St.
Fiorenzo, where report stated that a squadron of
the enemy's ships had been lately seen. The intelligence proved groundless—nothing was observed in
the gulf. The Minerve then stretched over to the
coast of France, to reconnoitre the harbour of
Toulon, off which the frigates remained two days,
although the Romulus, on the first of them, had the
misfortune to spring her mainmast and bowsprit:
six or seven French ships were lying in ordinary,
with only one frigate in a state for sea. From
Toulon the Minerve ran across the Gulf of Lyons
for Cape Creuse. Approaching the Spanish coast,
both frigates hoisted French colours, but no vessel
came out of Barcelona to speak them. Nothing
of interest offering in this quarter, the Commodore proceeded to the southward, with the intention
of looking into Mahon Harbour, but the wind
not serving, he stood along shore to Cape Palos,
in order to reconnoitre Carthagena ; near that port
a large ship was seen under the land, which either
did not think the British ships deserving of notice,

or had other objects in view to induce her not to
alter her course.

Looking into the harbour of Carthagena, two
frigates only were seen, and all doubt was thereby
removed of the Spanish grand fleet being at sea;
whether gone to the westward or to join the French
ships at Toulon, presented matter for conjecture.
The prevailing opinion was in favor of their having
gone for Cadiz; therefore the Commodore, after
satisfying his curiosity off Carthagena, decided to
push on to the westward. A fresh easterly breeze
taking the frigates off Cape de Gatt, and every acces-
sible port, in which the enemy could have taken
shelter, having been now explored, they stood mer-
rily on towards the Straits. The old Rock was soon
in sight, and on the afternoon of the 9th of February,
the Minerve and Romulus anchored off the new
mole in the bay of Gibraltar; and, as it singularly
chanced, a few hours before their arrival, the Southampton Division from Elba passed the Straits to
the westward; and the night following the Dido
and Sincere went through with their charge.

Commodore Nelson now learned that the Spanish
grand fleet had passed the Rock to the westward,
on Sunday the 5th of February, sending into the
bay of Gibraltar three two-deckers and a frigate
with supplies for the enemy's lines before Gibraltar:

these ships were still at anchor at the head of the
bay, near the Orange Grove.

It was soon ascertained that Lieutenants Culverhouse and Hardy were on board of one of the
Spanish men-of-war then in the bay. It will be
recollected, that these officers had been left in the
Sabina frigate, captured by the Minerve, on her
voyage to Porto Ferrajo, but afterwards abandoned
on the approach of a superior force. Negotiations
were opened to procure, if possible, their exchange,
as well as the exchange of the seamen who had been
made prisoners with them.

Governor O'Hara, then commanding the garrison,
earnestly pressed the Commodore to remain some
days at Gibraltar, but so anxious was Nelson to
rejoin Admiral Sir John Jervis, that he would not
hear of any longer period than was necessary to
obtain the exchange of the British officers and
seamen from the Spanish ships in the bay.

In the meantime, it had been decided to leave the
Romulus at Gibraltar, for the repairs she wanted.
In consequence of this arrangement, the gentlemen
of the Viceroy's suite who had been embarked in
that frigate were removed from her, and joined Sir
Gilbert in the Minerve, with which ship alone
Nelson now determined to proceed to join the Bri-
tish Admiral at the appointed rendezvous.

On the forenoon of the 11th of February, the
Minerve got under weigh. She had scarcely cast
round from her anchorage, when two of the three
Spanish line-of-battle ships in the upper part of
Gibraltar Bay were observed to be also in motion.
It was soon evident that they had been watching
the Commodore's movements, and were prepared to
pursue him as soon as the Minerve should take her
departure from Gibraltar.

As the Spanish ships had a steady wind from the
eastward over the Isthmus, whilst the Minerve was
embarrassed with the eddies and baffling flaws, that
usually prevail in an easterly wind, near the Rock,
the Spaniards had for some time the advantage in
pushing forwards in the bay. The Minerve was not,
however, long in getting the steady breeze, and soon
after got into the Straits, when the chace of the
enemy became, as we afterwards heard, a most interesting " spectacle" to our friends of the garrison.

The Minerve was a captured ship from the French
—taken in the Mediterranean in 1795, and considered to be a tolerably good sailer, particularly
with the wind on her quarter. The Spanish ships
were not equally good goers ; one of them, the
Terrible, was a first-rate sailer, well known to the
British officers, Culverhouse and Hardy, who had
been exchanged from her only the day before. Her
consort was a dull sailing ship. Advancing into

the Straits, the Minerve had the wind abaft, and
after marking her progress with that of the enemy,
it was evident that the headmost ship of the chace
gained on the British frigate.　No sooner was this
point ascertained, than directions were given by Sir
Gilbert Elliot to have certain parts of his public
papers ready to be sunk, if necessary, at a moment's
notice.　The ship was cleared for action, and the
position of the Minerve was now becoming every
moment more and more interesting.　At this period
I was walking with Commodore Nelson, conversing
on the probability of the enemy's engaging the
Minerve, and his words, and manner of uttering
them, made a strong impression on me.　He said
that he thought an engagement was very possible,
as the headmost ship appeared to be a good sailer;
but, continued he, (looking up at his broad pendant,) "before the Dons get hold of that bit of
bunting I will have a struggle with them, and
sooner than give up the frigate, I'll run her ashore."

Captain Cockburn, who had been taking a view
of the chacing enemy, now joined the Commodore,
and observed that there was no doubt of the headmost ship gaining on the Minerve.　At this moment
dinner was announced, but before Nelson and his
guests left the deck, orders were given to set the
studding sails.　At table I found myself seated next
to Lieutenant Hardy, and was congratulating him

on his late exchange from being a prisoner of war,
when the sudden cry of a "man overboard," threw
the dinner party into some disorder. The officers
of the ship ran on deck : I, with others, ran to the
stern windows to see if any thing could be observed
of the unfortunate man; we had scarcely reached
them before we noticed the lowering of the jolly
boat, in which was my late neighbour Hardy, with
a party of sailors ; and before many seconds had
elapsed, the current of the Straits (which runs
strongly to the eastward) had carried the jolly
boat far astern of the frigate, towards the Spanish
ships. Of course the first object was to recover,
if possible, the fallen man, but he was never seen
again. Hardy soon made a signal to that effect,
and the man was given up as lost. The attention
of every person was now turned to the safety of
Hardy and his boat's crew ; their situation was
extremely perilous, and their danger was every
instant increasing from the fast sailing of the headmost ship of the chace, which, by this time had
approached nearly within gun-shot of the Minerve.
The jolly boat's crew pulled "might and main" to
regain the frigate, but apparently made little progress against the current of the Straits. At this
crisis, Nelson, casting an anxious look at the
hazardous situation of Hardy and his companions,
exclaimed, "By G— I'll not lose Hardy ! Back the
mizen top-sail." No sooner said than done ; the

Minerve's progress was retarded, leaving the current to carry her down towards Hardy and his party, who seeing this spirited manœuvre to save them from returning to their old quarters on board the Terrible, naturally redoubled their exertions to rejoin the frigate. To the landsmen on board the Minerve an action now appeared to be inevitable; and so, it would appear, thought the enemy, who surprised and confounded by this daring manœuvre of the Commodore (being ignorant of the accident that led to it,) must have construed it into a direct challenge. Not conceiving, however, a Spanish ship of the line to be an equal match for a British frigate, with Nelson on board of her, the Captain of the Terrible suddenly shortened sail, in order to allow his consort to join him, and thus afforded time for the Minerve to drop down to the jolly-boat to take out Hardy and the crew; and the moment they were on board the frigate, orders were given again to make sail.

Being now under studding sails, and the widening of the Straits allowing the wind to be brought more on the Minerve's quarter, the frigate soon regained the lost distance; and, in a short time, we had the satisfaction to observe, that the dastardly Don was left far in our wake; and at sunset, by steering further to the southward, we lost sight of him and his consort altogether.

What course the Minerve pursued after night-
fall, I did not remark.   The interesting incidents
of the preceding day had afforded matter to occupy
our attention ; and we landsmen retired to rest,
congratulating ourselves on what we could not but
feel to have been a fortunate escape.

On the removal of the passengers from the Romulus into the Minerve, at Gibraltar, the crowded
state of the latter frigate would not allow of other
arrangements than of my having a cot slung alongside of that of the Viceroy, in the after cabin.   So
situated, I was awakened in the night, by the opening
of our cabin door, through which I saw, by the light
burning in the fore cabin, some person enter, and
on raising myself, I observed that it was Nelson.
Seeing me awake, he enquired if Sir Gilbert was
asleep, to which I replied in the affirmative.   To
my enquiry if any thing new had occurred, the Commodore approached my cot, and told me that he had
every reason to believe that the Minerve was at that
very moment in the midst of the Spanish fleet.   From
their signals, he said that he knew it was not that
of Sir John Jervis ; that the night was foggy ; that
the Minerve was then between two very large ships
within hail of each of them, and others were near
on all sides ; that he and Captain Cockburn had
little doubt of the strangers being Spanish ; that
Captain Cockburn and his officers were all on the

alert; and every cautionary direction given, particularly to watch the movements of the strange ships, and do as they did, &c., &c.

When Nelson had finished these details, I could not help observing that this was a verifying of the old adage, "out of the frying-pan into the fire," alluding to our escape of the day before. The Commodore allowed that we had got into something like a scrape, but added that it was quite unavoidable, on account of the night and fog; nevertheless, he thought that, with address, we might extricate ourselves.

He remained for some time, making various observations on these strange ships, and then continued to the following effect:—If they did not belong to the Spanish grand fleet, he thought they must be a convoy, or detached squadron, proceeding to the West Indies, (of which, it appears, he had received some previous information), and that, if the latter were the fact, they must be destined to strengthen the Spanish naval force in that quarter; in which case, it would be of the first moment that the British commander on the West India station should be early apprised of these movements of the enemy; a duty, he conceived he

c

was called upon to undertake, instead of joining Sir John Jervis.

On hearing Nelson express these opinions, I could not avoid saying, " But what will you do with Sir Gilbert Elliot ? it is of the greatest importance, owing to his recent interviews with the Italian states, that he should not only see Sir John Jervis, but reach England with the least possible delay." —The Commodore admitted the force of these remarks ; but the other point, in his judgment, outweighed every other consideration : "but," said he, breaking off, " I'll go on deck, and see how things are going on." To awake Sir Gilbert in our present uncertainty could answer no good purpose ; I therefore did not disturb him, but ruminated on this new and unlooked for occurrence, in the hope of devising some means of avoiding a trip to the West Indies, which, I thought would be at least an untoward conclusion of our Mediterranean campaign.

It soon occurred to me, that as we must pass near Madeira, in our way to the West Indies, the Viceroy and his party might be landed on that island ; or, if any neutral ship crossed our track, we might equally avail ourselves of a transfer to her, and obtain a passage to Lisbon, or perhaps to England.

This plan I had settled to my own satisfaction, when Nelson again appeared, and observed that the strange ships having been seen to tack, or wear, I forget which, the Minerve had followed their example ; and that after having so done, directions were given for the frigate's edging away insensibly, and that Captain Cockburn and himself were inclined to think the Minerve was getting out of the thick of the fleet, and would soon cease to be embarrassed with them. After this gratifying communication, Nelson repeated his former opinions and intentions, and we were earnestly discussing the subject, when Sir G. Elliot was awakened by our conversation. He was then made acquainted with all that had been passing, with the Commodore's suspicions regarding the strange ships, and with his conditional plan, to proceed immediately to the West Indies. After some general observations, and repeating his determination, if necessary, of carrying us to the West Indies, the Commodore left the cabin again, and soon returned with the agreeable intelligence that the Minerve had, he trusted, got quit of the strange fleet. " We propose," added Nelson, " to stand on our present course during the night : at daybreak, we shall take another direction, which will enable us to fall in with the strange ships again, should they be on their way to the westward. I shall then ascertain the force of the convoy, or of the squadron, if it consist only of men-of-war; and should it then appear advisable, I shall start for the West Indies. Should we not fall in with any strange ships in the course which the Minerve will steer after daybreak, my conclusion is, that the fleet we have fallen in with must be the grand fleet of Spain; it will be then of the first importance that I join Sir John Jervis as soon as possible, in order that he may be informed of the enemy's fleet not having been yet able to get into Cadiz, and of their state on quitting Carthagena, of which Lieutenants Culverhouse and Hardy are able to give the latest and most minute accounts."

The Commodore then left Sir Gilbert Elliot and me to our repose, if that were possible. After he had left the cabin, I asked Sir Gilbert what he thought of this new occurrence, and of the prospect of a trip to the West Indies. "It was another escape," he replied, "and as to the voyage to the West Indies, if the Commodore considered the public service required that proceeding, he must

submit to circumstances ; he was only a passenger."
This cool way of receiving and considering our present situation and prospects did not surprise me,
well acquainted as I was with the Viceroy's character. However, I made known to him the plan I
had devised to avoid a visit to a tropical climate,
of which he approved. Nothing further occurred
until we all met at breakfast, when the incidents of
the last twenty-four hours became the subject of
conversation, and were fully discussed. I then
learned that the Minerve was at that instant
standing on the course which would soon confirm
one of the two suspicions entertained by Nelson,
regarding the strange ships seen during the past
night. A good look out was naturally kept during
the whole of the 12th of February, but no ships of
any sort appearing, Nelson felt assured that the
fleet with which the Minerve had been entangled
the night before, was the Spanish grand fleet ; and
being more confirmed in this idea as the day
advanced, he became very anxious to join Sir John
Jervis's fleet, whose rendezvous, as fixed with the
Commodore, was not far from the place where we
then were.

At daybreak, on the 13th of February, the
weather was hazy, and as the Minerve was ap-

proaching the place of rendezvous, orders were
given for keeping a good look out. In the forenoon a brig and cutter hove in sight, and soon
after a larger sail, which, as the frigate neared,
was discovered to be a ship of war. She proved
to be the British frigate, the Lively, of thirty-two
guns, an out-skirter of Sir John Jervis's fleet, which
in a very short time the Minerve joined, not a little
to the gratification of all parties.

On joining Sir John Jervis's fleet, the Commodore, accompanied by the Viceroy, repaired on
board the flag-ship the Victory,—the latter to con-
fer with the Admiral on political matters, the former
to report in what manner he had executed his last
orders, and to communicate all the naval intelligence he had gleaned in his late cruize, particularly of his being chaced by the enemy on leaving
Gibraltar, and of his very recent nightly rencontre
with the Spanish grand fleet. It was at this period
that the capture of Lieutenants Culverhouse and
Hardy, so much regretted at the time it took place,
proved to be of the highest importance. The re-
captured Spanish frigate, Santa Sabina, in which
the above officers had been made prisoners, had
returned to Carthagena, where the greatest part of
the Spanish grand fleet was equipping for sea.

These English officers had thus many favorable opportunities of noticing their state and condition, and having also sailed with the fleet when it left Carthagena for Cadiz, they had ample means of obtaining accurate knowledge of their numbers, equipment, and discipline. The information collected by Lieutenants Culverhouse and Hardy was of the greatest value, and being made known to the British Admiral, was found to corroborate much of what he had learned from other quarters. Being also assured, not only by Nelson's intelligence, but by additional information brought by the Bonne Citoyenne, that the Spanish fleet was close at hand, Sir John Jervis, with that decision which was a prominent trait in his character, determined, notwithstanding the enemy's very superior force, to bring the Spaniards, if possible, to action.

No sooner was this decision taken, than the Admiral's intentions were promulgated to his squadron, by throwing out the signal to prepare for action. Nelson, on rejoining the fleet, quitted the Minerve, and resumed the command of his regular ship, the Captain. Sir Gilbert Elliot and his party also left the Minerve, and were directed to repair on board the Lively frigate, commanded by Lord Garlies, who had orders to proceed with them immediately to England. But the Viceroy could not bear the idea of leaving the British fleet at so critical and interesting a juncture. His Excellency's first request of Sir John Jervis was to be allowed to remain with the Admiral as a volunteer on board of the Victory, until the issue of the approaching contest was known, which proposal Sir John positively refused; and all that the Viceroy could obtain, was the Admiral's assent that the Lively should not leave the British fleet until she could carry with her the despatches conveying the result of the expected engagement.

This enabled me to be an eye-witness of the action of the 14th of February, 1797, and the following letter to my father contains the Narrative of that battle, which, as already mentioned, I published, on my arrival in England, in the spring of that year.

On board the Lively Frigate, off the Island of Scilly,

February 27, 1797.

Once more, my dear Sir, I am in sight of Old England, the land of rational liberty; and the pleasure of revisiting my native country, after an absence of six years, is not a little increased by the satisfaction of being on board a frigate that is the messenger of great and important news;—a splendid and decisive victory—a victory unparalleled in the annals of our naval history.

Admiral Sir John Jervis, with fifteen sail of the line and four frigates, has defeated the Spanish Grand fleet, consisting of twenty-seven ships of the line and ten frigates, and captured four sail of the line, two of which are of three decks.

This brilliant affair took place off Cape St. Vincent, on the 14th of February, the anniversary of St. Valentine, who by this glorious event has almost eclipsed his brother Crispian; and henceforth we must say, with the poet:

> " He *that's* outliv'd this day, and comes safe home,
> Will stand a tiptoe when the day is nam'd,
> And rouse him at the name of *Valentine*."

Captain Calder, Captain of the fleet under the command of Sir John Jervis, bears home the Admiral's dispatches, and is now on board the Lively. It is expected that he will land to-morrow; and I purpose to avail myself of that opportunity, to transmit you such an account of this splendid action, as I have been able to arrange in the time that has elapsed since we separated from the British fleet in Lagos Bay.

You will, perhaps, wish to know by what fortunate means I became a witness of this brilliant action; and, that my narrative may obtain the more credit with you, you shall be first satisfied on that head. When Sir Gilbert Elliot, late Viceroy of Corsica, embarked at Porto Ferrajo for England, I had the honour to accompany his Excellency. Sir Gilbert embarked on board the Minerve frigate, Captain George Cockburn, carrying the broad pendant of Commodore Nelson. We quitted Elba at the latter end of January, and, after reconnoitring the principal French and Spanish ports in the Mediterranean, arrived at Gibraltar a few days after the Spanish fleet had passed through the Straits from Carthagena. Impatient to join Admiral Sir John Jervis, Commodore Nelson remained only one day at Gibraltar, and proceeded from thence on the 11th of February to the westward. It is not essential to communicate to you the particulars attending the Minerve's being chaced by two Spanish line-of-battle ships from the Bay of Gibraltar; nor of her falling in with the Spanish fleet, off the mouth of the Straits. It is sufficient to say, the Commodore joined Admiral Sir John Jervis's fleet off Cape St. Vincent, on the 13th of February, just in time to communicate to the Admiral some interesting intelligence, concerning the force and state of the enemy's fleet, and to remove his pendant to the Captain, of 74 guns.

Upon joining the British fleet, the Lively frigate, commanded by the Right Hon. Lord Viscount Garlies, was appointed to proceed with Sir Gilbert Elliot, and the gentlemen accompanying him, to England; but there being at this time reason to expect an approaching action between the two fleets, the Lively, at the joint solicitations of Sir Gilbert Elliot and Lord Garlies, was detained with the squadron until the event should be known.

Thus stationed on board the Lively, which acted as a repeating frigate during the action, I was at liberty to observe the manœuvres of both fleets, and to view the interesting scene before me, with more precision and leisure than if the ship in which I was embarked had been a principal in the fight; and by comparing my notes with others, and conferring with the chief actors in this brilliant affair,

I have reason to believe, I have not only collected
correct information relative to the proceedings of
our fleet, and to the conduct of some individuals,
whose behaviour on that occasion entitles them
strongly to the admiration and gratitude of their
King and country ; but I am enabled to illustrate
my description of the events with a series of
sketches, shewing the fleets in various positions,
which to you who are conversant with my method,
and are interested in these details, will convey,
I have little doubt, a satisfactory idea of this
splendid and important engagement.

I need not, for the present purpose, detail to
you the many disappointments and unfortunate
accidents experienced by the British Admiral, previous to the moment which so amply repaid him
for all his former solicitude. Such a relation
would indeed strongly illustrate one of the great
qualities which so eminently distinguish his mind,
and would present him to you, not only firm and
undaunted, but rising under difficulties in proportion to their pressure. It will, however, be
sufficient for a clear comprehension of what I have
to lay before you, on the proceedings of the glorious
14th of February, to remark, that notwithstanding
the means taken by his Majesty's ministers for
augmenting Sir John's fleet to a force adequate
to the service, yet such had been the losses and

injuries* sustained by the British squadron, from
causes equally unavoidable and disastrous, that his
actual force, when the reinforcements, under the
command of Rear-Admiral William Parker, joined
him off Cape St. Vincent, was in effect the same
as that which he commanded when these reinforcements were first required. It is somewhat remark-
able, that even this force was in imminent danger
of being further diminished by the unfortunate
accident of the Colossus and Culloden running
aboard of each other, by which the latter received
such material and serious injury, that under any
other circumstances it might have been prudent
for her to have taken refuge in the nearest port.
The zeal, activity, and resources of her commander,
Captain Troubridge, were however equal to the
remedying of this evil; and in a short time the
Culloden, though her damages could by no means
be entirely repaired, was nevertheless reported fit
again for service.

With some commanders it might have been

---

* Courageux, of 74 guns, lost in the Straits of Gibraltar.

Gibraltar, of 80 guns, forced from her anchorage at Gibraltar, struck
on the Pearl Rock in quitting the Bay, and obliged to proceed to
England for repairs.

Zealous, of 74 guns, struck on a rock in Tangiers Bay, and obliged
to repair at Lisbon.

Bombay Castle, of 74 guns, lost in going into the River Tagus.

Saint George, of three decks, grounded on the Cachops, coming out
of the Tagus the 18th January, and obliged to put back for repairs.

deemed the most prudent conduct, under these circumstances, to have acted on the defensive until additional ships had been sent from England : with Sir John Jervis it was otherwise—he, confiding in the unanimity, zeal, and bravery of the squadron under his command, determined on active operations. Fixing a rendezvous for his reinforcements, for his cruisers, and for the convoys that he expected, he went to sea with ten sail of the line, though he knew the enemy might have, if they had not, thrice that number ; and after accompanying a Portuguese squadron and convoy a convenient distance to the westward, he repaired to the place appointed, where he was joined by his reinforcement, under Rear-Admiral Parker.

Before I enter on the detail of the proceedings of the important day which will certainly immortalize the name of Jervis, and of his brave seconds, it is proper to state the relative force of the British and Spanish fleets.

The British fleet, or to use, I believe, a more correct term, the British squadron, consisted of fifteen sail of the line, four frigates, a sloop of war, and a cutter ; viz., two of 100 guns, two of 98 guns, two of 90 guns.—Total, six three-deckers, eight of 74 guns, and one of 64 guns.*

* *Vide* Appendix, No. II.

The Spanish fleet was composed of twenty-seven sail of the line, ten frigates, and one brig; viz., one of four decks, carrying 136 guns; six of three decks, each of 112 guns; two of 84 guns, and eighteen of 74 guns each.*

The Spanish Admiral had sailed from Carthagena the 4th February. On the 5th, he passed Gibraltar, leaving in that Bay three line-of-battle ships, supposed to be laden with military stores for the Spanish troops stationed before that garrison; two of which ships afterwards chaced Commodore Nelson, in the Minerve. The strong easterly gale that had been friendly for their getting out of the Mediterranean, was however unpropitious to their gaining the Port of Cadiz.

On the night of the 11th, as I have before mentioned, they were fallen in with, off the mouth of the Straits, by the Minerve. And the evening of the day on which Commodore Nelson joined Sir John Jervis off Cape St. Vincent, we find their fleet driven farther to the westward; for a part of them were not only seen by the Minerve, before she joined the British fleet, but La Bonne Citoyenne, a British sloop of war, commanded by Captain Lindsay, arrived in the fleet the same evening with intelligence, that not two hours before she had exchanged

* *Vide* Appendix, No. III.

shots with one of the enemy's frigates, and that the enemy's fleet was not far distant.

It was upon receiving this intelligence, and hearing Sir John Jervis, in consequence of it, give orders for the signal to be made to prepare for battle, that Sir Gilbert Elliot and Lord Garlies earnestly solicited to remain with the squadron until the event of the action should be known; and his consent to this request enables me to offer you a detail of the operations of that day, so highly honorable to the British arms.

And now, my dear Sir, having satisfied you on my own means of information, I proceed to the object of my letter.

Before sun-set in the evening of the 13th, the signal had been made for the British squadron to prepare for battle, and the ships were also directed to keep in close order during the night.

At daybreak on the 14th (St. Valentine's day) the British fleet was in complete order, formed in two divisions (*vide* plate No. 1,) standing on a wind to the S. S. W.   The morning was hazy.   About half-past six o'clock, A.M., the Culloden made the signal for five sail in the S. W. by S. quarter, which was soon after confirmed by the Lively and Niger frigates, and that the strange sail were by the wind on the starboard tack. The Bonne Citoyenne sloop of war, Captain Lindsay, was therefore directed to reconnoitre. At a quarter past eight o'clock, the squadron was ordered, by signal, to form in a close order; and in a few minutes afterwards the signal was repeated to prepare for battle.

About half-past nine o'clock, the Culloden, Blenheim, and Prince George, were ordered to chace in the S. by W. quarter; which, upon the Bonne Citoyenne's making a signal that she saw eight sail in that quarter, was afterwards strengthened by the Irresistible, Colossus, and Orion.

A little past ten o'clock, the Minerve frigate made the signal for twenty sail in the S. W. quarter, and a few minutes after, of eight sail in the S. by W. Half an hour afterwards the Bonne Citoyenne made the signal that she could distinguish sixteen, and immediately afterwards twenty-five of the strange ships, to be of the line. The enemy's fleet were indeed become now visible to all the British squadron.

The ships first discovered by the Culloden, were separated from their main body, which being to windward, were bearing down in some confusion, with a view of joining their separated ships. It

appeared to have been the British Admiral's intention, upon discovering the separated ships of the
enemy's fleet, to have cut them off, if possible, before
their main body could arrive to their assistance;
and, with this view, the fast sailing ships of his
squadron were ordered to chace.

Assured now of the near position of their main
body, he probably judged it most advisable to form
his fleet into the line of battle, and the signal was
made for their forming the line of battle a-head and
a-stern as most convenient. A signal was made
directing the squadron to steer S. S. W. (*Vide*
plate No. II.)

About twenty minutes past eleven o'clock, the
Admiral pointed out that the Victory (his flag-ship)
would take her station next to the Colossus.   Some
variation in steering was afterwards directed, in
order to let the rear ships close up.   At twenty-six
minutes past eleven o'clock, the Admiral communicated his intention to pass through the enemy's line,
hoisting his large flag and ensign, and soon after
the signal was made to engage.

The British van by this time had approached the
enemy ; and the distinction of leading the British
line into action, fell to the lot of the Culloden,
commanded by Captain Troubridge.   About half-

past eleven o'clock, the firing commenced from the Culloden against the enemy's headmost ships to windward.

As the British squadron advanced, the action became more general; and it was soon apparent that the British Admiral had accomplished his design of passing through the enemy's line.

The animated and regular fire of the British squadron was but feebly returned by the enemy's ships to windward, which, being frustrated in their attempts to join the separated ships, had been obliged to haul their wind on the larboard tack: those to leeward, and which were most effectually cut off from their main body, attempted also to form on their larboard tack, apparently with a determination of either passing through, or to leeward of our line, and joining their friends; but the warm reception they met with from the centre ships of our squadron, soon obliged them to put about; and excepting one, the whole sought safety in flight, and did not again appear in the action until the close of the day, (*vide* plate No. III).

The single ship just mentioned persevered in passing to leeward of the British line, but was so covered with smoke, that her intention was not discovered until she had reached the rear, when she was not permitted to pass without notice, but received the fire of our sternmost ships; and as she luffed round the rear, the Lively and other frigates had also the honor of exchanging with this two-decker several broadsides.

Sir John Jervis, having effected his first purpose, now directed his whole attention to the enemy's main body to windward, consisting at this time of eighteen sail of the line.   At eight minutes past twelve, the signal therefore was made for the British fleet to tack in succession, and soon after he made the signal for again passing the enemy's line.

The Spanish Admiral's plan seemed to be to join his ships to leeward, by wearing round the rear of our line; and the ships which had passed and exchanged shots with our squadron, had actually borne up with this view.

This design, however, was frustrated by the timely opposition of Commodore Nelson, whose place in the rear of the British line afforded him an opportunity of observing this manœuvre, and of penetrating the Spanish Admiral's intention. His ship, the Captain, had no sooner passed the rear of the enemy's ships that were to windward, than he ordered her to wear, and stood on the other tack towards the enemy.

In executing this bold and decisive manœuvre, the Commodore reached the sixth ship from the enemy's rear, which was the Spanish Admiral's own ship, the Santissima Trinidad, of 136 guns, a ship of four decks, and said to be the largest in the world. Notwithstanding the inequality of force, the Commodore instantly engaged this colossal opponent, and for a considerable time had to contend not only with her, but with her seconds a-head and a-stern, of three decks each. While he maintained this unequal combat, which we viewed with admiration mixed with anxiety, his friends were flying to his support, (*vide* plate No. IV.); and the enemy's attention was soon directed to the Culloden, Captain Troubridge, and in a short time after to the Blenheim, of 90 guns, Captain Frederick, who opportunely came to their assistance.

The intrepid conduct of the Commodore staggered the Spanish Admiral, who already appeared to waver in pursuing his intention of joining the ships cut off by the British fleet, when the Culloden's arrival, and Captain Troubridge's spirited support of the Captain, together with the approach of the Blenheim, followed by Rear-Admiral Parker, with the Prince

George, Orion, Irresistible, and Diadem, not far distant, determined the Spanish Admiral to change his design altogether, and to make the signal for the ships of his main body to haul their wind, and make sail on the larboard tack.

Advantage was now apparent in favor of the British squadron, and not a moment was lost in improving it. As the ships of Rear-Admiral Parker's division approached the enemy's ships, in support of the Captain and her gallant seconds, the Blenheim and Culloden, (*vide* plate No. V.) the cannonade became more animated and impressive. The superiority of the British fire over that of the enemy, and its effects on the enemy's hulls and sails, were so evident, that we in the frigate no longer hesitated to pronounce a glorious termination of the contest.

The British squadron at this time was formed in two divisions, both on the larboard tack; their situation was as follows : (*vide* plate No. VI.) Rear-Admiral Parker, with the Blenheim, Culloden, Prince George, the Rear-Admiral's ship, Captain, Orion, Irresistible, composed one division, which was engaged with the enemy's rear. Sir John Jervis, with the other division, consisting of the Excellent, Victory, Barfleur, Namur, Egmont,

Goliah, and Britannia, was pressing forward in support of his advanced squadron, but had not yet approached the real scene of action.

The Colossus having, in the early part of the day, unfortunately lost her fore-yard and fore-top-sail-yard, was obliged, in consequence of these losses, to fall to leeward, and the Minerve's signal was made to take her in tow, which was, however, handsomely declined by Captain Murray, when the Minerve had come within hail in execution of her orders.

While the British advanced division warmly pressed the enemy's centre and rear, the Admiral meditated, with his division, a co-operation, which must effectually compel some of them to surrender.

In the confusion of their retreat, several of the enemy's ships had doubled on each other, and in the rear they were three or four deep, (*vide* plate No. VI.) It was therefore the British Admiral's design to reach the weathermost of these ships, then bear up, and rake them all in succession with the seven ships composing his division. His object afterwards was to pass on to the support of his van division, which, from the length of time they had been engaged, he judged might be in want of it. The casual position, however, of the rear ships of his van division, prevented his executing this plan:

the Admiral, therefore, ordered the Excellent, the leading ship of his own division, to bear up; and, with the Victory, he himself passed to leeward of the enemy's rearmost and leewardmost ships, which, though almost silenced in their fire, continued obstinately to resist the animated attacks of all their opponents.

Captain Collingwood, in the Excellent, in obedience to the Admiral's orders, passed between the two rearmost ships of the enemy's line, (*vide* plate No. VI.) giving to the one most to windward, a seventy-four, so effectual a broadside, that, with what she had received before, her captain was induced to submit. The Excellent afterwards bore down on the ship to leeward, a three-decker; but observing the Orion engaged with her, and the Victory approaching her, he threw into her only a few discharges of musketry, and passed on to the support of the Captain, at that time warmly engaged with a three-decker carrying a flag. His interference here was opportune, as the continual and long fire of the Captain had almost expended the ammunition she had at hand, and the loss of her fore-top-mast, and other injuries she had received in her rigging, had rendered her nearly ungovernable.

The Spanish three-decker had lost her mizen-mast; and before the Excellent arrived in her

proper station to open on this ship, the three-decker
dropped astern aboard of, and became entangled
with, a Spanish two-decker that was her second:
thus doubled on each other, the Excellent gave the
two ships her fire, and then moved forwards to
assist the headmost ships in their attack on the
Spanish Admiral, and the other ships of the enemy's
centre.

Meanwhile, Sir John Jervis, disappointed in his
plan of raking the enemy's rear ships, and having
directed, as before observed, the Excellent to bear
up, ordered the Victory to be placed on the lee-
quarter of the rearmost ship of the enemy, a three-
decker, (*vide* plate No. VI.) and having, by signal,
ordered the Irresistible and Diadem to suspend
their firing, threw into the three-decker so powerful
a discharge, that her commander, seeing the Barfleur, carrying Vice-Admiral the Hon. W. Walde-
grave's flag, ready to second the Victory, thought
proper to strike to the British chief.   Two of the
enemy's ships had now surrendered, and the Lively
frigate and Diadem had orders to secure the prizes.
The next that fell, were the two with which Commodore Nelson was engaged.

While Captain Collingwood so nobly stepped in
to his assistance, as has been mentioned before,
Captain R. W. Miller, the Commodore's Captain,

was enabled to replenish his lockers with shot, and
prepare for a renewal of the fight : no sooner, therefore, had the Excellent passed on, than the gallant
Commodore renewed the battle.

The three-decker with which he was before engaged having fallen aboard her second, that ship, of
84 guns, became now the Captain's opponent. To
her Commodore Nelson directed a vigorous fire ;
nor was it feebly returned, as the loss of the Captain
evinced, near twenty men being killed and wounded
in a very few minutes. It was now that the various
damages already sustained by that ship through the
long and arduous conflict which she had maintained,
appearing to render a continuance of the contest in
the usual way precarious, or perhaps impossible ;
and the Commodore not bearing to part with an
enemy of whom he had assured himself, he instantly
resolved on a bold and decisive measure, and determined, whatever might be the event, to attempt his
opponent sword in hand. The boarders were sum-
moned, and orders given to lay the Captain on
board the enemy.

Fortune favors the brave ; nor on this occasion
was she unmindful of her favorite. Captain Miller
so judiciously directed the course of the Captain,
that she was laid aboard the starboard quarter
of the eighty-four gun ship, (*vide* plate No. VI.)

her spritsail yard passing over the enemy's poop,
and hooking her mizen shrouds; and the word to
board being given, the officers and seamen destined
for this duty, headed by Lieutenant Berry, together
with the detachment of the 69th regiment, commanded by Lieutenant Pearson, then doing duty
as marines on board the Captain, passed with
rapidity on board the enemy's ship; and in a
short time the San Nicolas was in the possession
of her intrepid assailants. The Commodore's impa-
tience would not permit him to remain an inactive
spectator of this event. He knew the attempt was
hazardous; and his presence, he thought, might
contribute to its success. He therefore accompanied the party in this attack, passing from the
fore chains of his own ship into the enemy's quarter
gallery, and thence through the cabin to the
quarter-deck, where he arrived in time to receive
the sword of the dying commander, who was mor-
tally wounded by the boarders. For a few minutes
after the officers had submitted, the crew below
were firing their lower-deck guns: this irregularity,
however, was soon corrected, and measures taken
for the security of the conquest. But this labor
was no sooner achieved, than he found himself
engaged in another and more arduous one. The
stern of the three-decker, his former opponent,
was directly amidships on the weather-beam of the
San Nicolas; and, from her poop and galleries,

the enemy sorely annoyed, with musketry, the
British on board the San Nicolas. The Commodore was not long in resolving on the conduct
to be observed upon this momentous occasion. The
alternative that presented itself, was to quit the
prize, or advance. Confident in the bravery of
his seamen, he determined on the latter. Directing
therefore an additional number of men to be sent
from the Captain, on board the San Nicolas, the
undaunted Commodore headed himself the assailants in this new attack, and success crowned the
enterprise. Such, indeed, was the panic occasioned
by his preceding conduct, that the British no sooner
appeared on the quarter-deck of their new opponent, than the Commandant advanced, and asking
for the British commanding officer, dropped on one
knee, and presented to him his sword; making, at
the same time, an excuse for the Spanish Admiral's
not appearing, as he was dangerously wounded.
For a moment Commodore Nelson could scarcely
persuade himself of this second instance of good
fortune; he therefore ordered the Spanish Commandant, who had the rank of a Brigadier, to
assemble the officers on the quarter-deck, and direct
steps to be taken instantly for communicating to
the crew the surrender of the ship. All the officers
immediately appeared, and the Commodore found
the surrender of the San Josef ascertained, by each
of them delivering to him his sword.

The Coxswain of Nelson's barge had attended
him throughout this perilous adventure. To his
charge the Commodore gave the swords of the
Spanish officers as he received them; and the
jolly tar, as they were delivered to him, tucked
these honorable trophies under his arm, with all
the *sang-froid* imaginable.

It was at this moment also that an honest Jack
Tar, an old acquaintance of Nelson's, came up
to him in the fulness of his heart, and excusing
the liberty he was taking, asked to shake him
by the hand, to congratulate him upon seeing
him safe on the quarter-deck of a Spanish three-
decker.

H. M. S. CAPTAIN BOARDING THE SAN NICOLAS, ETC.

This new conquest had scarcely submitted, and the Commodore returned on board the San Nicolas, when the latter ship was discovered to be on fire in two places. At the first moment appearances were alarming; but presence of mind and resources were not wanting to the British officers in this emergency. The firemen were immediately ordered from the Captain; and proper means being taken, the fires were soon got under.

A signal was now made by the Captain, for boats to assist in separating her from her prizes; and as the Captain was incapable of further service until refitted, the Commodore hoisted his pendant, for the moment, on board the Minerve frigate, and in the evening removed it to the Irresistible, Captain Martin.

Four of the enemy's ships were now in possession of the British squadron (two of three decks, the Salvador del Mondo, and the San Josef, of 112 guns each; one of 84, the San Nicolas; and the San Ysidro, of 74 guns;) and the van of the British line still continued to press hard the Santissima Trinidad, and others in the rear of the enemy's flying fleet. The approach, however, of the enemy's ships which had been separated from their main body in the morning, two new ships also bearing down from to windward, (*vide* plates,

No. VI. and VII.) and two of the enemy's flying
ships wearing to support their chief, at that time
severely pressed, (*vide* plate, No. VII.) add to
which, the closing of the day—these circumstances,
but more particularly the lateness of the hour,
while the prizes were not yet properly secured,
determined the British Admiral to bring to. The
headmost of the enemy's approaching ships (in all
nine in number, two of which were of three decks)
had indeed advanced to fire on the Britannia, in
which Vice-Admiral Thompson carried his flag,
and the sternmost ships of the rear-division, which
were fortunately, at this period, in a situation to
keep the enemy in check. The Victory likewise,
with the Barfleur and Namur, had formed to cover
the prizes. The British Admiral, therefore, a little
before four o'clock, P.M., made the preparative, and
soon after the signal for the British fleet to bring to.
The enemy's fresh ships, on approaching, opened
a fire on our covering ships; but, though both
fresh, and so superior in numbers, (*vide* Plate,
No. VII.) they contented themselves with the noise
of a few irregular broadsides, leaving their captured
friends, and seeming too happy to be allowed to
escape with their discomfited chief, and his disabled
companions, to think of molesting our squadron in
bringing to on the starboard tack.

The frigates having orders to take in charge

the prizes not already taken possession of, the four were soon secured as well as circumstances permitted; and the Captain having suffered very considerably in her masts and rigging, the Minerve was ordered to take her in tow.

H M. S. CAPTAIN IN TOW OF THE MINERVE.

At the close of the evening, the British fleet was again formed in most admirable line of battle, on a wind with their heads to the southward, (*vide* plate No. VIII.) and the Niger frigate ordered to look out during the night.

The close of the day, before the four prizes were secured, undoubtedly saved the Spanish Admiral's flag from falling into the hands of the victors. The Santissima Trinidad, in which he carried it, had been so much the object of attention, that the ship was a perfect wreck when the action ceased. Many indeed aver, that she actually struck both her flag and ensign, hoisting a flag as a signal of submission ; but as she continued her course, and afterwards hoisted a Spanish jack, others doubt this circumstance. It is however, a truth, that her fire had been silent for some time before this event is reported to have occurred.

The loss of the enemy in this engagement must have been very considerable. The fire of the British squadron was, throughout the action, superior in the proportion of five or six to one ; and if we were to judge from the number of killed and wounded found on board the prizes, their casualties must greatly exceed the numbers that have been usually computed. Almost all their wounded that had lost limbs died for want of assistance ; and many others, who were wounded in other parts, were found dead in the holds.

The loss of the British squadron, in killed and wounded, * amounted to exactly three hundred : moderate indeed, when compared with that of the enemy, and considering the duration of the action ! But the expenditure of ammunition was, I am told, beyond any recent example. The Culloden expended, it is said, one hundred and seventy barrels

* *Vide* Appendix No. I.

E

of powder; the Captain, one hundred and forty-six;
and the Blenheim, one hundred and eighty; other
ships expended in the same proportion. It is not
unworthy of remark also, that not a single gun in
the British squadron burst in this action.

The Captain fired more shot than are usually
given to a ship of her rate, at her first equipment
in England; and it was observed, that when shot
or grape were wanting on board this ship for the
carronades, the tars substituted in their place nine-
pounds shot, seven of which were frequently dis-
charged at one time, and then at so short a distance, that every shot of the seven must have had
effect.

I could wish, my dear Sir, in this place, to convey
to you, in some adequate manner, the merits of the
chief personages in this glorious transaction; but
the praise of those who were most conspicuous will,
after all, be best collected from this faithful narrative
of their actions: it is far above the power of my
pen to express. I confess, the admiration with
which I viewed their conduct would not permit me
to be silent, or to suppress the strong feelings
excited in my mind, by all the glories of that memorable day,—if it were not for a real despair of
reaching the extraordinary merits of some,—and
for a sincere apprehension of doing injustice, even to

those whom I might name, as well as to those whom I might from ignorance omit. Certain it is, that while the Admiral, and some distinguished actors in this scene, are covered with never-fading laurels, —if others of the squadron had not the same important share in the operations of the day, it was owing to circumstances not dependent on themselves, and to no want of ardour or personal exertion.

If I may be permitted to hazard an opinion, the whole squadron have gained immortal honor; for the victory of the 14th of February stands, in all its circumstances, first and unparalleled in naval history.

The Spanish fleet, from our best accounts, consisted of twenty-seven sail of the line, and ten frigates : several of them, however, had no share in the action until the close of the day; and after the British Admiral had passed through their line, little more than their main body ever renewed the fight. It was a defensive combat entirely on their part, after Commodore Nelson obliged them to haul their wind on the larboard tack.

Their fleet appeared to be most indifferently manned; the flag ships had not more than sixty or eighty seamen on board, the remainder of their crews consisting of pressed landsmen, and soldiers of their new levies. It does not seem to have been their intention to seek the British squadron; nay, we have reason to think they would have been happy to have avoided them, notwithstanding their superiority: but the British Admiral availed himself of the haze of the morning to surprise them. Their object, since the 5th of the month, had been to reach the port of Cadiz, but contrary winds (the strong easterly gale) had driven their fleet so far to the westward; and the very morning of the action, before they had discovered the British squadron, the signal, I am told, had been made for bearing up for that port, in consequence of a favorable change of wind during the preceding night.

Some of the prisoners spoke very reasonably and sensibly on the operations and events of the day. In general, they were inclined to admit that the Spanish fleet was not in a proper state to appear at sea; and some of them, in the ill-humour of a defeat, observed that it was not an uncommon thing, before the fleet quitted Carthagena, to hear both misfortune and disgrace predicted, if their fleet were to meet even an inferior force of British ships. An officer of one of the prizes said, that on board the ship in which he served, it was impossible, after the first broadside, for the captain or officers to persuade any of the crew to go aloft to repair the injured rigging : threats and punishment were equally ineffectual. He had seen some severe examples made for disobedience of orders ; but though two or three had been killed, and several wounded, these severities had no effect. The panic-struck wretches, when called upon to go aloft, fell immediately on their knees, and, in that posture, cried out, that they preferred being sacrificed on the spot, to performing a duty in the execution of which they considered death as inevitable.

On board the San Josef, when the British sailors had taken possession, it was remarked by the English officers, that four or five tompions were still fixed in the quarter deck guns of the side that had been engaged ; and the reason being demanded, the people on board replied, with a shrug of the shoulders, that the animated and destructive cannonade of the British ships had not allowed them to fire these guns. It is a question, indeed, if they were loaded. It was observed also, by several of the advanced division of the British squadron, that as soon as their guns were run out to repeat a broadside, the enemy appeared, to them, invariably to quit their guns ; and, it is thought, threw themselves prostrate on the decks, to escape, if possible, the effects of the discharge.

Thus, my dear Sir, you have the most interesting

particulars of this brilliant affair.   I have other
anecdotes in store; which I reserve until we meet
to talk over this, as well as other occurrences, that
have happened since we parted.   I cannot, however, conclude my letter without remarking, for your
satisfaction, knowing you to be a particular man,
that the time mentioned in the narrative is taken
from the minutes kept on board the VICTORY.
Some difference occurs between them and those
kept on board other ships; but I have thought
proper to follow the former, conceiving them to be
the most correct.   In the hope of our meeting in a
few days, I remain,

MY DEAR SIR, &c.

J. DRINKWATER.

THE CAPTURED SALVADOR DEL MUNDO IN TOW OF H. M. S. NAMUR.

APPENDIX.

APPENDIX.

No. I.

RETURN of the KILLED and WOUNDED, on board the BRITISH SQUADRON, commanded by Admiral SIR JOHN JERVIS, K. B., in the Action with the SPANISH FLEET, off Cape St. Vincent, on the 14th of February, 1797.

Ships' Names.	Guns.	KILLED.		WOUNDED.		Officers' Names, killed or wounded.
		Officers	Seam. Sold. & Marines.	Officers.	Seam. Sold. & Marines.	
Captain . . 74	74	1	23	2	54	Major Wm. Norris, marines, killed. Mr. James Goodenech, midsh. ditto. Commodore H. Nelson bruised, but not obliged to quit the deck. Mr. Carrington, boatswain, wounded in boarding the San Nicolas. Mr. Thomas Lund, midsh. wounded.
Blenheim . . 90	90	0	12	2	47	Mr. Edw. Libby, acting lieutenant, wounded. Mr. Peacock, boatswain, wounded. Mr. Joseph Wrixon, master's mate, wounded, since dead.
Culloden . . 74	74	1	9	0	47	Lieut. Livingstone, marines, killed.
Excellent . . 74	74	1	10	0	12	Mr. P. Peffers, boatswain, killed. Mr. E. A. Doune, master's mate, wounded.
Irresistible . 74	74	0	5	1	13	Serjeant Watson, marines, killed. Lieut. A Thompson, wounded. Mr. W. Balfour, midship. wounded. Mr. H. M'Kinnon, master's mate, wounded.
Prince George 98	98	0	8	0	7	
Orion . . . 74	74	0	0	0	9	Mr. Thomas Mansel, mid. wounded.
Goliah. . . 74	74	0	0	0	8	
Namur . . 90	90	0	2	0	5	
Barfleur . . 98	98	0	0	0	7	
VICTORY . .100	100	0	1	0	5	
Colossus . . 74	74	0	0	0	5	
Diadem . . 64	64	0	0	0	2	
Britannia. .100	100	0	0	0	1	
Egmont . . 74	74	0	0	0	0	
Total -	-	3	70	5	222	

Total killed and wounded—300.

No. II.

NAMES of the SHIPS composing the BRITISH SQUADRON, under the command of Admiral Sir JOHN JERVIS, K. B., on the 14th of February, 1797, disposed in the temporary order of battle.

No.	Ships' Names.	Guns.	Commanders.
1	Blenheim	90	T. L. Frederick.
2	Diadem	64	G. H. Towry.
3	Prince George . .	98	{ Rear Admiral W. Parker. { T. Irwin.
4	Irresistible . . .	74	G. Martin.
5	Britannia	100	{ Vice-Admiral Thompson. { T. Foley.
6	Captain	74	{ Commodore H. Nelson. { R. W. Miller.
7	Egmont	74	J. Sutton.
8	VICTORY	100	(Admiral Sir John Jervis, K. B. { ——— R. Calder. (——— G. Grey.
9	Culloden	74	T. Troubridge.
10	Orion	74	Sir James Saumarez.
11	Colossus	74	G. Murray.
12	Barfleur	98	{ Vice-Admiral Hon. Wm. Waldegrave. { J. R. Dacres.
13	Excellent	74	C. Collingwood.
14	Goliah	74	Sir C. H. Knowles, Bart.
15	Namur	90	J. H. Whitshed.

Total . . 1232 guns.

Difference against the British Fleet, 1076 guns.

FRIGATES.

	Guns.	Commanders.
Lively	32	Rt. Hon. Lord Viscount Garlies.
La Minerve . . .	40	G. Cockburn.
Niger	32	E. J. Foote.
Southampton . . .	32	J. M'Namara.
La Bonne Citoyenne .	18	C. Lindsay.
Raven Brig . . .	18	W. Prowse.
Fox Cutter	12	Lieut. Gibson.

No. III.

NAMES of the SHIPS composing the SPANISH FLEET, under the command of Vice-Admiral DON JOSEPH CORDOVA, on the 14th of February, 1797, in the action with the BRITISH SQUADRON, off Cape St. Vincent; copied from a list of their line of battle, found on board the San Ysidro, after she struck.

No.	Ships' Names.	Guns.	Frigates' Names.	Guns.
	Van Squadron			
1	Bahama	74		
2	Pelayo	74		
3	San Pablo	74	Brigida	34
4	Neptuno	84	Casilda	34
5	Concepcion	112	Perla	34
6	San Domingo	74	Mercedes	34
7	Conquistador	74		
8	San Juan Nepomuceno	74		
9	San Genaro	74		
	Centre Squadron			
10	Mexicano	112		
11	Terrible	74		
12	Oriente	74	Paz	34
13	Soberano	74	Dorotea	34
14	SANTISSIMA TRINIDAD	136	Guadalupe	34
15	San Nicolas	84 (taken)	Santa Teresa	34
16	San Ysidro	74 (ditto)	Vigilante (Brig)	12
17	Salvador del Mondo	112 (ditto)		
18	San Ildefonso	74		
	Rear Squadron			
19	Conde de Regla	112		
20	San Firmin	74		
21	Firme	74	Matilda	34
22	Principe de Asturias	112	Diana	34
23	San Antonio	74	Atocha	34
24	Glorioso	74	Ceres	34
25	Atlante	74		
26	San Francisco de Paula	74		
27	San Josef	112 (taken)		

Total . . . . . 2308 guns.

Difference in favor of the Spanish Fleet, 1076 guns.

REFERENCE TO PLATE I.

Shewing the Positions of the British and Spanish Fleets, when several Ships of the Spanish Fleet were first discovered by the British.

————

A. British Fleet in the order of sailing in two divisions.

B. La Bonne Citoyenne, sloop of war, Captain Lindsay, advanced a-head, and to windward of the British Fleet, to reconnoitre.

C. Several Spanish ships and frigates first discovered by the British Fleet.

D. Supposed position of the main body of the Spanish Fleet, at this time obscured by the fog of the morning.

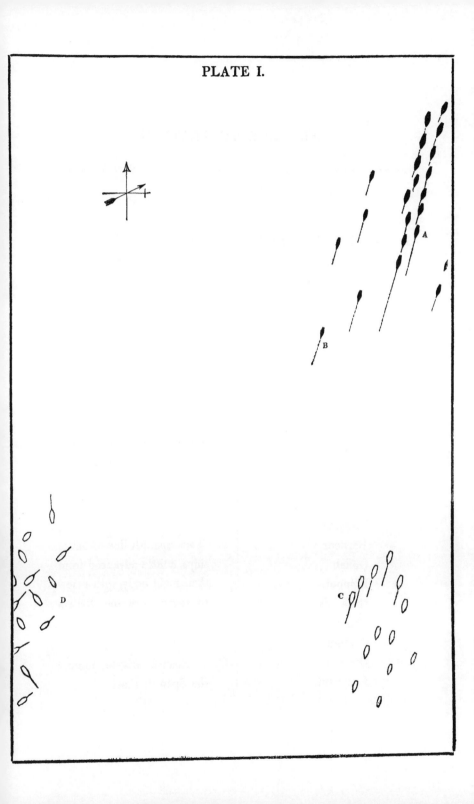

PLATE I.

REFERENCE TO PLATE II.

Shewing the Position of the British and Spanish Fleets about half-past Eleven o'clock, A.M.

A. The British Fleet formed in line of battle, as most convenient, on the starboard tack, advancing to cut off the Spanish ships that were separated from their main body.

BRITISH LINE OF BATTLE.
Culloden.
Blenheim.
Prince George.
Orion.
Irresistible.
Colossus.
VICTORY.
Barfleur.
Goliah.
Egmont.
Britannia.
Namur.
Captain.
Diadem.
Excellent.

B. British frigates bearing up to pass to leeward of their Fleet.

C. Several Spanish line-of-battle ships and frigates separated from their main body, and standing away on the starboard tack.

D. The main body of the Spanish Fleet, bearing down in a confused manner to support their ships to leeward.

E. Two Spanish line-of-battle ships, a little advanced from their main body, with a view to reconnoitre the British Fleet.

G. A Spanish frigate joining the Spanish Fleet.

PLATE II.

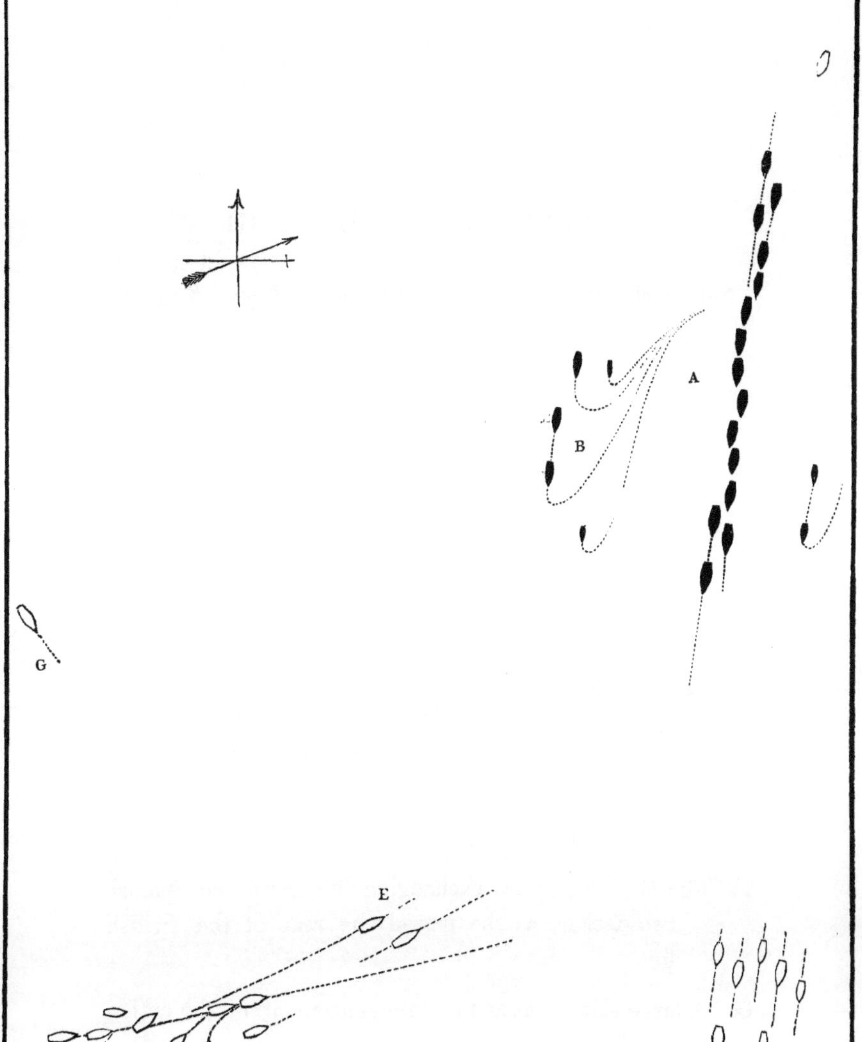

REFERENCE TO PLATE III.

————

A. British Fleet passing through the Enemy's line.

B. Culloden tacking to engage the enemy's main body to windward.

C. Main body of the Spanish Fleet, which, after passing the British Fleet on the larboard tack, bore up with an apparent design of joining their ships to leeward.

D. Spanish ships cut off from their main body, attempting to join their friends, but obliged to wear and sheer off by the superior force of the British fire.

E. A Spanish line-of-battle ship, which succeeded in joining the main body.

F. The British frigates exchanging fires with the Spanish two-decker, as she passed the rear of the British line.

G. A large ship, that at the commencement of the action set all sail, and soon disappeared to leeward.

PLATE III.

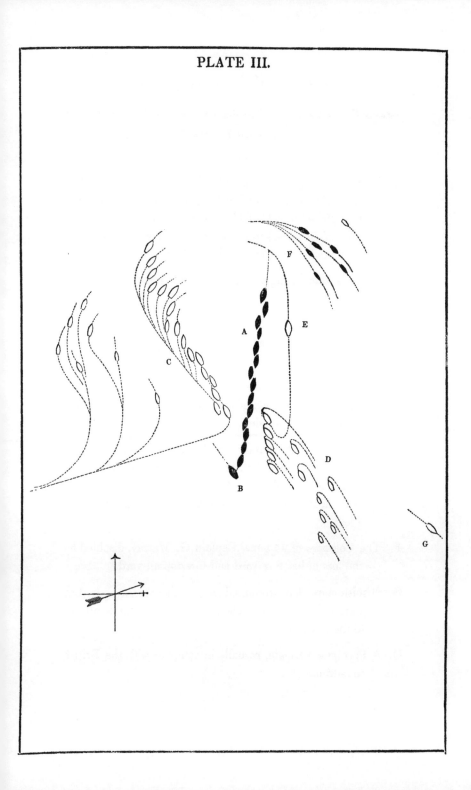

REFERENCE TO PLATE IV.

Shewing the Positions of the British and Spanish Fleets about three quarters past Twelve o'clock.

A. The main body of the Spanish Fleet hauling their wind on the larboard tack, and making sail in consequence of the spirited attack of Commodore Nelson, in the Captain, of 74 guns, supported by the Culloden, of 74 guns, commanded by Captain Troubridge.

B. The Captain engaged with the Santissima Trinidad, of 136 guns, and two other three-decked ships, which were seconds to the Spanish Admiral.

C. The Culloden, engaged with the rear ships of the Enemy's main body.

D. The Blenheim, a three-decker, of 90 guns, commanded by T. L. Frederick, advancing to the assistance of the Captain and Culloden.

E. Rear-Admiral W. Parker, in the Prince George, of 98 guns; with the Orion, of 74 guns; Irresistible, of 74 guns; and Diadem, of 64 guns; approaching to support the attack on the centre and rear of the Enemy's Fleet.

F. The Colossus, of 74 guns, Captain G. Murray, disabled by the loss of her fore-yard and fore-topsail-yard.

G. Spanish ships that attempted to join their main body, but were obliged to sheer off, and afterwards made all sail to the southward.

H. A Portuguese frigate, casually in company with the British squadron.

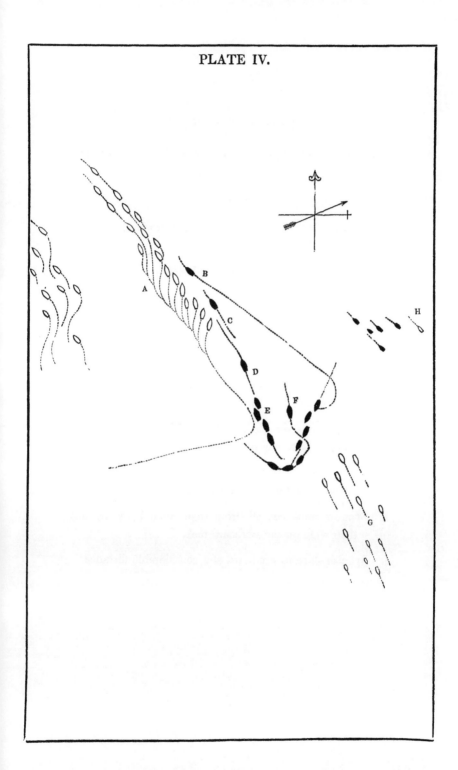

PLATE IV.

REFERENCE TO PLATE V.

*Shewing the Positions of the British and Spanish Fleets about half-past
One o'clock, P.M.*

———

A. Enemy's Fleet making off in great confusion on the larboard tack.

B. The Blenheim, Capt. T. L. Frederick ⎤

C. The Captain, Commodore Nelson— ⎟ Closely engaged
   Captain R. W. Miller. ⎬ with the enemy's
                                        ⎟ centre and rear.
D. The Culloden, Captain Troubridge ⎦

E. Rear-Admiral W. Parker, with the Prince George, Orion, Irresistible, and Diadem, commencing the action with the rear ships of the Enemy.

F. The Colossus disabled, and the Minerve frigate approaching to her assistance.

G. The Victory, with the remainder of the British Fleet, close hauled on the larboard tack.

H. Spanish ships cut off from their main body, hauling their wind on the starboard tack.

I. Spanish ships to windward at a considerable distance.

PLATE V.

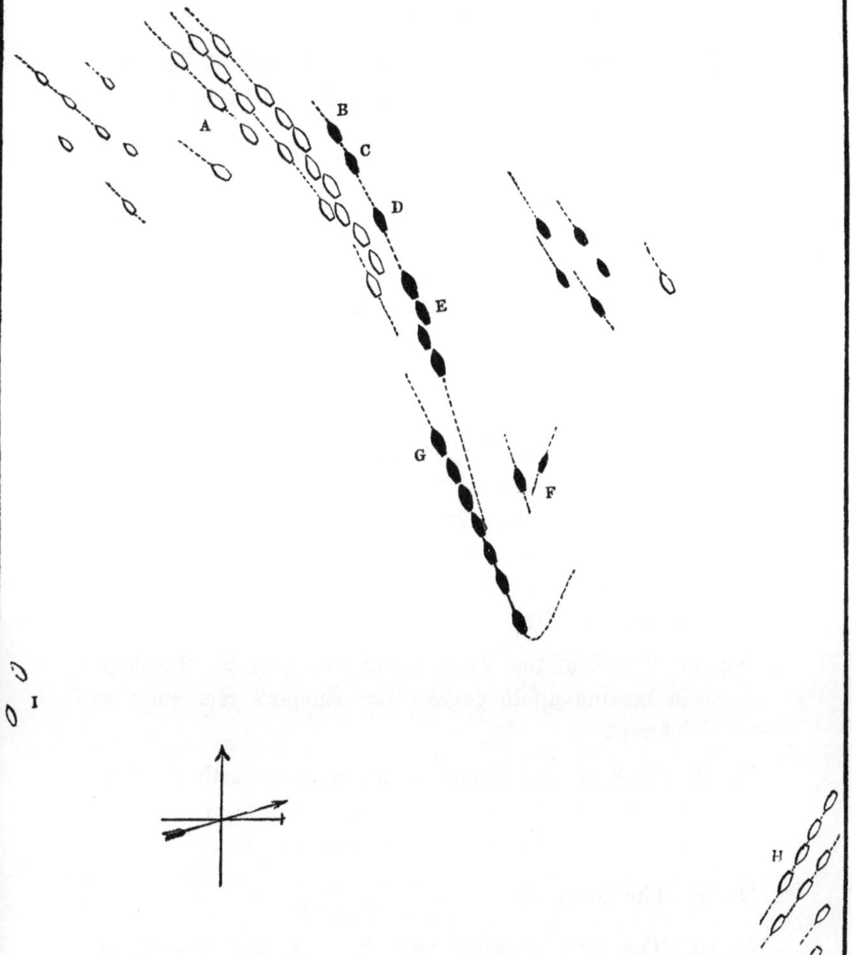

REFERENCE TO PLATE VI.

Shewing the Positions of the British and Spanish Fleets from half-past Two o'clock to half-past Three o'clock, P.M.

A. The advanced Division of the British Fleet, consisting of the Blenheim, Culloden, Prince George, Captain, Orion, Irresistible, and Diadem.

B. The rear Division, consisting of the Excellent, VICTORY, Barfleur, Namur, Egmont, Goliah, and Britannia.

C. The Colossus.

D. The main body of the Spanish Fleet, making off in confusion.

E. Spanish ships which had been cut off from their main body in the morning, now rejoining their friends.

F. Two Spanish line-of-battle ships, not seen at the commencement of the action, now approaching from to windward.

No. 1. Track of the Excellent, when Captain Collingwood bore up, and passed between the San Isidro, No. 2, and the Salvador del Mundo, No. 3, to the support of the Captain, No. 4, and the ships engaged with the Santissima Trinidad, No. 5, and others of the Enemy's centre.

No. 6. Track of the Victory, and No. 7, of the Barfleur, in bearing up to engage the Enemy's rear ships to leeward.

No. 8. Track of the Namur, which bore up with the Victory and Barfleur, but afterwards luffed up to oppose the Enemy's fresh ships and cover the prizes.

No. 9. The Britannia.

No. 10. The San Nicolas, and No. 11, the San Josef, which were boarded, and carried sword in hand, by Commodore Nelson, in the Captain.

PLATE VI.

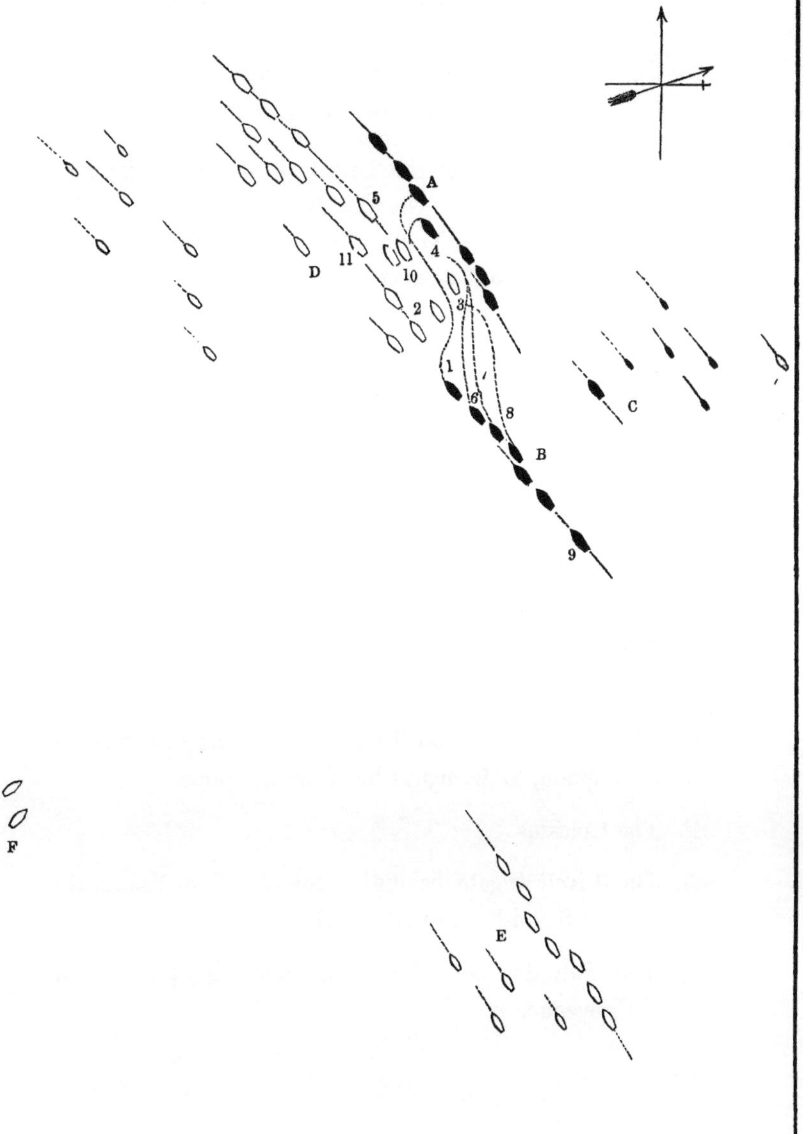

REFERENCE TO PLATE VII.

Shewing the Positions of the British and Spanish Fleets, about three quarters past Three o'clock, P.M.

A. The rear Division of the British Fleet, viz., Britannia, No. 1; Goliah, No. 2; Barfleur, No. 3; Victory, No. 4; Namur, No. 5; Excellent, No. 6; Egmont, No. 7; covering the prizes, and the injured ships of the advanced Division, against the Enemy's fresh ships, arrived to support their Admiral-in-Chief.

B. The Santissima Trinidad on the eve of striking, if not already struck.

C. Two line-of-battle ships of the Enemy's van wearing, on the junction of the reinforcement of fresh ships, to support their Chief.

D. The Captain, entangled with her two prizes, the San Nicolas and San Josef.

E. The Diadem (64), and the Minerve frigate, assisting the Captain, to disengage her from her prizes.

F. The Colossus.

G. The Lively frigate having in tow the San Ysidro, the first Spanish ship that struck.

H. The Salvador del Mondo, attended by the Bonne Citoyenne.

PLATE VII.

REFERENCE TO PLATE VIII.

Shewing the Positions of the British and Spanish Fleets on the evening of the 14th of February.

———

A. The British Fleet formed in a line of battle a-head, the prizes and disabled ships being to leeward in tow of the frigates.

B. The Spanish Fleet to windward, in great confusion.

C. The Niger frigate, Captain Foote, the look-out of the British Fleet.

PLATE VIII.

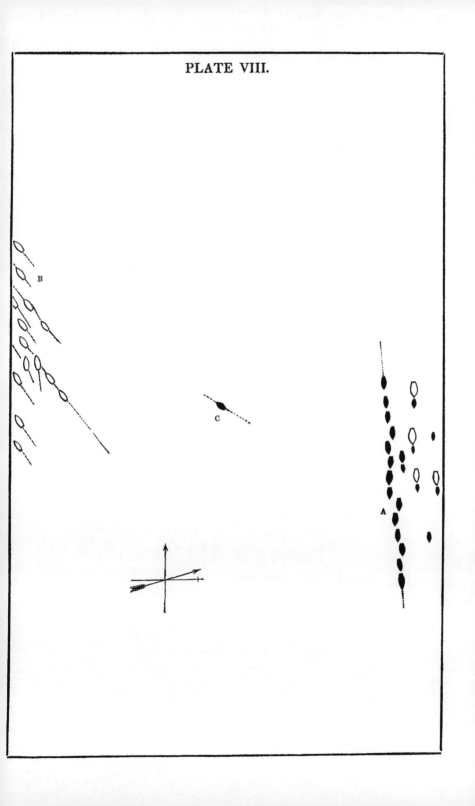

IN the preceding Narrative of the Battle of St. Vincent, are given the principal transactions of that glorious day—a day which, in point of weather, seemed to be made for the purpose. In the early part it was hazy, and thus concealed the British squadron and their movements; with no more wind than to allow the ships to go into action under top-gallant sails. There was no sea, and as the day advanced, the haze dispersed, to show the enemy's fleet in two bodies—the main division to windward, in great disorder, and the British squadron in one compact line a-head, executing with precision a bold manœuvre to confound and discomfit their opponents. From sunrise to sunset the day was occupied with the most interesting and momentous occurrences, and it closed with the proud triumph of defeating a force, superior in numbers more than three to two, and capturing four sail of the line.

Sir Gilbert Elliot and his party were all assembled in the Lively frigate on the 13th, and on the following—the day of battle, the passengers so collected had stations and duties allotted to them in the frigate during the action;—even the Viceroy had his charge.

When the leeward division of the Spanish fleet was first discovered, and afterwards engaged and cut off from joining their main body, all those ships, except one, put before the wind and made sail. The single ship thus excepted, wore and stood on the other tack, with the design of passing round the rear of the British ships, and of joining her friends in the main body to windward, which intention she accomplished in the manner already mentioned. Her course lay between the British line-of-battle ships and the British frigates. In passing to windward of the latter, she presented so tempting an object to the Lively, that the gunner, an old seaman, was very anxious to be at her. Lord Garlies at first opposed this, until at length the gunner was so importunate to have one shot from a favorite gun, an eighteen-pounder in the midships, which he assured his lordship he was certain would hit the Don, that Lord Garlies consented to his request, and the old fellow, as well as all on board, was much gratified to see the shot strike the two-decker, near the fourth or fifth porthole abaft. We were afterwards informed that this shot killed and wounded four or five men, for in the after action, this ship, the San Ysidro, became a prize, and the Lively was ordered to take possession of her. Finding herself thus within our range, the San Ysidro gave the Lively and the other frigates her broadside; but so badly were the guns pointed,

that not one shot struck our ships, though many
went through their sails. Several British frigates
joined the Lively in returning the Spaniard's fire for
a few rounds, but she soon got out of reach, and our
attention in the Lively was, by that time, called to
a more interesting object—that of H. M. ship
Captain, carrying the broad pendant of our friend
Nelson, lying alongside of, and under a Spanish
four-decker, the *Santissima Trinidad*, the enemy's
flag-ship in chief, and two other three-deckers ; and
dealing out a rapid, incessant, and destructive fire
amongst her colossal opponents. The contest in
which the Commodore was thus engaged, appeared
to us so unequal, and the contrast between the
Captain, a small 74-gun ship, and the gigantic ships
of the enemy, was so preposterous, that we could, at
the moment, only view this proceeding of Nelson
as rash and perilous in the extreme. With this
exception of the Captain, the orderly conduct
and regular manœuvres of the rest of the British
squadron at this moment, gave their movements
more the appearance of a naval review than a
deadly fight between two powerful fleets. It was
only the falling of yards and masts, the disorder of
sails and rigging, and other marks of destruction,
that assured us landsmen in the Lively, aloof from
the heat of the actual battle, that the action before
our eyes was real. To myself, who thus, for the
first time, was a spectator of a naval engagement, the

scene before me was uncommonly interesting. The
animation, cheerfulness, and exertions of the Lively's
crew, officers and men, throughout the whole of
the day's business, could not but attract my special
notice and admiration; and the exhilaration was
contagious, for all on board seemed to be equally
excited by the proceedings of the day.

Victory at length was decided in favor of the
British squadron, by the surrender of several of the
enemy's ships. The first that struck was the San
Ysidro, of 74 guns, of which the Lively was ordered
to take possession. When the Spanish commander
was brought on board the Lively, he presented his
sword to Lord Garlies, the captain of the frigate,
who very handsomely desired it might be tendered
to his illustrious passenger, the late Viceroy of
Corsica, Sir Gilbert Elliot, to whom the ensign of
the captured ship was likewise given by Lord
Garlies.

All the gentlemen of the Viceroy's party were
presented with trophies of the capture, consisting of
swords and pistols. A musquetoon, or iron blunder-
buss, called a *trabuca*, which had been used in the
battle in one of the tops, attracted my notice, and
became my memorial of the fight: it was a rude and
novel weapon, and is still preserved and exhibited
as a family token of triumph.

Three other prizes were soon afterwards secured by the British squadron, and I am convinced the Spanish Admiral-in-Chief's ship, the Santissima Trinidad, of 130 guns, should have been added to the number. In the original narrative, I mentioned the circumstance doubtfully, although I can affirm that, in an interval of the clearing away of the smoke, I saw a white flag flying over the Spanish ensign, importing her surrender. I mentioned the fact to those near me at the time; but the discomfited ship, being at that moment supported by the division of eight ships cut off in the morning, but which had now rejoined their friends to windward, drifted away under their protection—dismasted, and a log on the water. Such was her crippled state, that she was allowed to separate from the main body of the enemy's fleet, and was seen (as was reported before the Lively left the British squadron) alone, off Cape St. Mary's, making the best of her way into port, where she eventually arrived. Many years, however, did not elapse before the same Santissima Trinidad became a prize to the Hero, who engaged her so gallantly on the 14th of February, in the still more memorable and tremendous battle off Cape Trafalgar, in October, 1805.

On the morning of the 15th of February, the two hostile fleets were in sight of each other, both nearly

becalmed, Cape St. Vincent bearing from the British
fleet about N. A large ship was seen to the eastward, attended by a frigate, which, it was con-
jectured, was the disabled Santissima Trinidad. A
signal was made for the Namur to chace in that
quarter, which was soon after annulled, in consequence, as it was supposed, of the Admiral not
thinking it prudent to lose the services of so powerful a ship, (the Namur was of 90 guns,) whilst the
enemy's fleet, still very superior in numbers, had the
option, being to windward, of renewing the action.

On the morning of the 15th, Sir Gilbert Elliot
proceeded to offer to the British Admiral his congratulations on the success of the previous day.
Lord Garlies of course accompanied him. I was to
have been of this party, and was actually descending
the side ladder, when, being in uniform, it was discovered that I was without side-arms, for which I
returned ; but, when I got back to the gangway, the
place destined for me was occupied by another
person. My friends kindly offered to make room
for me, but as this could not be done without occa-
sioning great inconvenience to the whole party, I
reluctantly gave up the intention of accompanying
them.

My disappointment, however, was amply made
up by what took place immediately after the

Lively's barge had left the frigate. A boat was seen approaching the Lively on the opposite side, and I heard with surprise, and no little pleasure, that Nelson was on board of her. Seeing me on the quarter-deck, the Commodore immediately approached me, offering his hand, which I seized with a most cordial grasp, expressing, at the same time, my high admiration of the gallant conduct of the Captain on the preceding day, and my warmest congratulations on the success of the battle.

" Where is Sir Gilbert?" was his first inquiry. " Gone with Lord Garlies to the Victory," was my reply.—" I hoped," he rejoined, " to have caught him before he saw the Admiral, but come below with me," and he led the way to the cabin.

Seated alone with the Commodore, I renewed in the most expressive terms, my congratulations on his safety from the perils of such a fight, and on the very distinguished part he had personally taken in the action, of which many particulars had by this time reached the Lively. He received my compliments with great modesty, though evidently with great satisfaction. I then remarked that, as the Lively would bear the glorious news to England, I should feel much obliged by his giving me as many particulars of the proceedings of his ship, the Captain, and of his own conduct in the capture of the two ships, as he was disposed to communicate. Our intimacy was such, that I felt no difficulty in drawing from him these details ; and this circumstance will be an apology for my making these remarks with such great freedom. I observed to him, that the position of the Captain appeared to all of us in the Lively, to be for a long time most extraordinary and unaccountable. We had expected every instant to see the ship annihilated by the overpowering force to which she was singly opposed. In the animation of conversation, I went so far as to ask, "How came you, Commodore, to get into that singular and perilous situation?" He good-naturedly replied, "I'll tell you how it happened. The Admiral's intention, I saw, was to cut off the detached squadron of eight sail, and afterwards attack the main body, weakened by this separation. Observing, however, as our squadron advanced and became engaged with the enemy's ships, that the main body of the enemy were pushing to join their friends to leeward, by passing in the rear of our squadron, I thought, unless by some prompt and extraordinary measure, the main body could be diverted from this course, until Sir John (at that time in action in the Victory) could see their plan, his well arranged designs on the enemy would be frustrated. I therefore ordered the Captain to wear, and passing the rear of our squadron, directed Captain Miller to steer for the centre of the enemy's fleet, where was their Admiral-in-Chief, seconded by two three-deckers, hoping by this proceeding to confound them, and, if possible, make them change their course, (as he did,) and thus afford Sir John Jervis time to see their movements, and take measures to follow up his original intention."—I do not say that Nelson expressed himself in exactly the above words, but his statement was to the same effect.*

* I have since often heard Commodore Nelson's conduct, in the above transaction, variously commented on. According to the strict rules of discipline, some persons say the Captain should not have quitted the British line-of-battle without orders. The strength of Sir John Jervis's squadron lay in its compactness, and the loss of one ship, from any cause, where the numbers opposed to each other were so disproportionate, might have defeated the British Admiral's manœuvres, and even have endangered the safety of the whole. Others have remarked, and apparently with good grounds, that when Nelson saw the necessity of some immediate and bold measure to disconcert the enemy, and had decided on the step he took, he should not have gone alone, but have taken with his own seventy-four, all the ships in his rear; and if we may judge from results, and the success of one ship, there can be no doubt that the attack of the Captain, supported by two or three others, must have been more effective, and the victory of the day would, in that case, have been more complete. In these comments there seems to be reason and good sense; but in warfare, circumstances must often arise which baffle principles, and customary modes of proceeding. Nelson, no doubt, saw the conduct of the Spanish Admiral in its true light: his decision and boldness astonished and confounded the enemy, who were thus taken by surprise, and unprepared for such singular resolution. The measure succeeded, and to this movement, hazardous as it was, may chiefly be attributed the success of the day.

In compliance with my request, he then gave
me the details of his boarding the St. Nicholas,
and afterwards the St. Josef, which are given
in the original Narrative, adding the following
particulars :—" I saw (and then he spoke with
increased animation) that from the disabled state
of the Captain, and the effective attack of the
approaching British ships, I was likely to have
my beaten opponent taken from me; I therefore
decided to board the St. Nicholas, which I had
chiefly fought, and considered to be my prize.
Orders were given to lay the Captain aboard of
her : the spritsail-yard passed into her mizen rigging. Lieutenant Berry with the ship's boarders,
and Captain Pearson with the 69th regiment,
(acting as marines on board the Captain,) soon
got possession of the enemy's ship. Assisted by
one of the sailors, I got from the fore-chains into
the quarter-gallery through the window, and thence
through the cabin to the quarter-deck, where I
found my gallant friends already triumphant." He
then gave me the details of the extraordinary circumstances attending his afterwards getting possession of the St. Josef. Of course, my high
admiration of his conduct was often expressed,
as he proceeded, in giving me these very interesting
particulars, of which I made pencil notes on a
scrap of paper I found at hand ; and these commu-
nications from my gallant friend were the more

valuable, from their being made before he had seen any other officer of the fleet, except Captain G. Martin, of the Irresistible, to which ship he had repaired for refreshment and repose, until the Captain, his own ship, almost a wreck in her rigging, &c., could be put into manageable order.

Towards the conclusion of this interesting interview, I repeated my cordial felicitations at his personal safety, after such very perilous achievements. I then adverted to the honors that must attend such distinguished services. " The Admiral," I observed, " of course will be made a peer, and his seconds in command noticed accordingly. As for you, Commodore," I continued, " they will make you a baronet." The word was scarcely uttered, when placing his hand on my arm, and looking me most expressively in the face, he said, " No, no : if they want to mark my services, it must not be in that manner."—" Oh !" said I, interrupting him, " you wish to be made a Knight of the Bath," for I could not imagine that his ambition, at that time, led him to expect a peerage. My supposition proved to be correct, for he instantly answered me, " Yes ; if my services have been of any value, let them be noticed in a way that the public may know me—or them." I cannot distinctly remember which of these terms was used, but, from his manner, I could have no

doubt of his meaning, that he wished to bear about
his person some honorary distinction, to attract the
public eye, and mark his professional services.

This casual discovery of Nelson's peculiar feelings
on this subject was not forgotten, or without conse-
quences. As was expected, his Majesty, in reward
for Nelson's distinguished conduct, had intended to
create him a baronet. Sir Gilbert Elliot, who took
a warm interest in Nelson's welfare, called on me in
London to impart this news; when I made known
to him the purport of my conversation on board the
Lively, and suggested that it was advisable to make
this circumstance known to the government. Sir
Gilbert saw the matter in the same light. He lost
no time in communicating what had passed on
this subject to some member of the cabinet, Lord
Spencer, I believe, who was then at the head of the
Admiralty Board, and his lordship took steps to
meet Nelson's wishes, in the manner most likely to
gratify his feelings, by obtaining for him, instead of
a baronetcy, the Order of the Bath, although, for
that purpose, it was necessary to make him an
extra knight.

What I had noticed in the above interview with
Nelson, agreed perfectly with the opinion I formed
from all I observed during our subsequent acquaintance. The attainment of public honours, and an

ambition to be distinguished above his fellows, were his master passions. His conduct was constantly actuated by these predominant feelings. It will account for the personal gratification he invariably evinced at receiving the many decorative honors presented to him by almost every power in Europe in amity with Great Britain; but, in reference to such distinctions, it may be observed, that if such pre-eminent talents as those of this most extraordinary man could be so cheaply purchased, the English nation, and indeed Europe, situated as she then was, had only to approve and applaud his moderation. *

* But how short-sighted we mortals are! These decorative honors, of which Commodore Nelson was so proud as even not to lay them aside in moments of active hostility, were, no doubt, the cause of his death.

Lord Nelson was covered with decorations on the day of the battle of Trafalgar, and thus became an object for a humble sharp-shooter to mark out, and, by a fatal rifle-ball, to deprive his country of one of its most distinguished and fortunate commanders.

Relating, not long ago, the above anecdote to an acquaintance, he told me that his family, whilst residing in the neighbourhood of Paris, after the general peace of 1815, employed a French artificer who was on board the French ship, the Redoubtable, in the battle of Trafalgar. This man professed himself to be an intimate friend of the man who, from that ship, killed Lord Nelson, and who was then living in Paris. According to his account, the attention of his shipmate had been attracted, during the battle, to an officer in the Victory, whom, from the decorations he wore, he suspected to be the British Admiral. Under this impression, the man obtained four ball-cartridges, with which, and his rifle, he went aloft, saying to his companions—" Si je ne le tue pas de ces trois, je me brûle la cervelle avec la quatrième." If this man's story is to be believed, the report of some officer on board the Victory having killed the man who shot Nelson, must be unfounded.

When Nelson quitted the Lively, he went on board the Victory, to receive from his gallant Chief, Sir John Jervis, and from his friend, Sir Gilbert Elliot, those congratulations and commendations which he so highly merited.

There being little wind on the 15th of February, both fleets, as has been already remarked, remained almost becalmed in sight of each other. That of the enemy appeared in great disorder; the British squadron was concentrated. On the 16th, the British squadron was still off Cape St. Vincent, which, on account of the adverse wind, and the disabled state of the prizes, the squadron could not weather. If they could have passed to the westward of the

It is well known that Nelson was buried in the Cathedral of St. Paul's, but it may not be known why St. Paul's Cathedral was preferred to Westminster Abbey, which, according to the generally received rumour of the day, had been named by Nelson himself as his ultimate place of rest. "Westminster Abbey or a golden chain," are words attributed to the gallant hero, on one of the many occasions when he was about to attempt some hazardous service; but there must be an error in putting these words in his mouth, for amongst his intimate friends, it was generally understood that he had imbibed some unaccountable objection to being buried in the Abbey. No doubt, his mortal remains would have been deposited there, surrounded by innumerable British heroes like himself, and other eminent public men, had not government been apprised of Nelson's peculiar opinions and feelings on this subject. It was in deference to this antipathy, that the place of interment was changed from Westminster Abbey to St. Paul's Cathedral, where, as a special mark of distinction, Nelson's body is placed in a vault constructed under the centre of the beautiful dome.

Cape, it was thought the Admiral would have proceeded to Lisbon.

During the day, some movements of the enemy indicating an intention of approaching the British squadron, Sir John, closely attentive to their proceedings, ordered the frigates to assemble round the Victory, to be at hand to act towards the prizes (which, in case of a renewal of hostilities, might embarrass him) in such manner as circumstances might point out.

Various reports were in circulation regarding their disposal in case of another action. Amongst other measures, it was rumoured that it had been suggested to run the four prizes ashore on the coast of Portugal, and to leave the Spanish crews to shift for themselves. All conjecture on this head was, however, removed in the afternoon: finding it not practicable to get round Cape St. Vincent, the Admiral made the signal to bear away for Lagos Bay, a few leagues to leeward, where the squadron and the prizes came to anchor in the evening.*

* On the fleet's assembling in Lagos Bay, the Admiral communicated, in general orders, his thanks to the admirals and officers of the squadron under his command, in the following terms:—

"Victory, Lagos Bay,
"Sir,   February 16, 1797.

"No language I am possessed of can convey the high sense I entertain of the exemplary conduct of the flag-officers, captains, officers,

On the 17th, despatches were sent off by land
to Lisbon, giving information of the late victory.
In the course of the day, intelligence reached Sir
John, through an American trader, that a large
three-decker, supposed to be the Santissima Trinidad, had been seen off Cape St. Mary's, in
distress, with an English frigate hovering round
her. Two frigates were in consequence detached
to bring her in, or to destroy her; but although
the disabled ship proved to be the ship in question,
her crew at length contrived to get her into port.

The 18th of February proved to be calm, but a
fine day. The Spanish fleet had now approached
Cape St. Vincent, off which they were seen, in

seamen, marines, and soldiers, embarked on board every ship of the
squadron I have the honor to command, present at the vigorous and
successful attack made upon the fleet of Spain on the 14th inst. The
signal advantage obtained by His Majesty's arms on that day, is entirely
owing to their determined valor and discipline; and I request you will
accept yourself, and give my thanks and approbation to those composing
the crew of the ship under your command.

" I am, Sir,

" Your most humble Servant,

" J. JERVIS."

"To ———, Captain
of H. M. Ship ———."

Considering how distinguished had been the services of some of the
commanders of the fleet in the action of the 14th, it was thought extraordinary at the time, that not the least notice, by name, was taken of
any of these officers in the preceding circular communication to the
squadron.

number, twenty-two ships of the line, manœuvring, as well as they were able, to form a line-of-battle.

Arrangements having by this time been made with the Portuguese authorities at Lagos, for the reception of the Spanish prisoners of war, they were landed this day, to the number of about 2300 men, and commenced their march to the eastward for the Spanish frontier. In the afternoon, a large Spanish frigate that had hugged the shore, under cover of a small headland, forming the western point of the Bay of Lagos, suddenly appeared, almost within shot of the British squadron. The Lively's signal was made to slip and chace, but the enemy no sooner saw his danger, than he hauled his wind, and, crowding all sail, stood for the Spanish fleet, then drawing off from the land, and the Lively's signal was annulled. At night, two of the British frigates were chaced into the anchorage of the fleet, by one of the enemy's line-of-battle ships. On Sunday, the 19th of February, Captain Robert Calder, captain of the fleet, came on board the Lively, with the Admiral's despatches, of which he was to be the bearer to England. About noon, the Lively got under way, and the wind having become favorable, and blowing fresh, she soon doubled Cape St. Vincent, seeing nothing of the Spanish fleet, and before night-fall, had left the British squadron far behind.

H

The Lively lay her course towards England until
the 23rd of February, when the wind changed to
the eastward.   On the 25th, she had got into
soundings, but the adverse easterly wind prevented
her advancing up the Channel.   By the 28th, the
Lively had weathered the Scilly Islands, and passed
to the northward, between those islands and the
Lands End.   There being little prospect of any
change of wind, and Captain Calder being very
impatient to reach London with his good news, he
desired Lord Garlies to put him on shore at St.
Ive's, where he landed, giving express orders that
no letters, nor any other person except himself and
servant should be allowed to land.   Some idea was
then entertained that the Lively might make for
Milford Haven, but our good fortune interposed to
defeat this project, which, had it been carried into
effect, might have brought the frigate into contact
with a French flying squadron, then hovering off
the coast of South Wales, and which had landed a
body of troops near Fishguard.   It was luckily decided to return to the English Channel, where the
frigate contrived to contend for some days against
a stiff Levanter, until she had got abreast of the
Eddystone, when seeing little prospect of any alteration in the wind, and anxious to get on shore, Sir
Gilbert Elliot requested Lord Garlies to land him
and his party at Plymouth ; and, in a few hours after
our course was changed, I had the satisfaction

(which is only to be felt and understood by those who have been absent long on foreign service) of finding myself once more in old England.

We landed on Sunday, the 5th of March. Being the messengers of such glorious news as the defeat of the Spanish grand fleet, the rumour of which, it was concluded, would have already reached Plymouth, we anticipated a most joyful reception. We expected, on our reaching the shore, that the Lively's arrival would have been hailed with the customary congratulations and rejoicings; but the people who received us, did not even enquire whence she came. Not a word nor a sign of welcome met our landing. Captain Calder had kept his good news so secret, that not a whisper of it had reached Plymouth, where, not a little to our surprise, we saw nothing but long faces and desponding looks in all classes.

We were not, however, long in learning the cause of this appearance and behaviour. Before we could tell them our gratifying intelligence, they announced to us the news (which had reached them that morning from the metropolis) of the shutting up of the National Bank of England, and the general *suspension of cash payments*. The union of the Spanish with the French fleets, they added, was considered as certain. Some flying

squadrons of the latter were then known to be
in the Irish channel, and the usual alarm of invasion universally prevailed. Nothing but England's
disgrace and downfall was foretold and talked of
throughout the kingdom.

After listening to these discouraging details for
some time, we availed ourselves of the first favorable
opening to relieve them of some of their apprehen-
sions. Immediate invasion, we said, was not to be
looked for. Sir John Jervis had retarded, if not
entirely defeated that measure ; and we then made
known the particulars of the glorious Battle of
St. Valentine's day. For some time they would
scarcely give our statements credit ; and even when
at length the fact was forced on their belief, such
was the panic then prevailing, that we could only
collect at Plymouth, from the Admiral, the General,
and other friends, fifteen guineas in gold, towards
enabling the Viceroy, and his party of six individuals, and their servants, to pay their travelling
expenses to the metropolis.

I cannot better conclude these anecdotes than by
recording a conversation which I had with Nelson
on the very next occasion of my seeing him. After
the battle of St. Vincent, it is well known that
he was actively employed in the bombardment of
Cadiz, and subsequently detached on a special

service to Santa Cruz, in the island of Teneriffe, where he met with the injury which caused him the loss of his right arm. He had returned to England, and was still suffering severely from the effects of the amputation, when I was allowed to see him. This was just before the victory of Camperdown, and intelligence of interest was hourly expected to arrive from Admiral Duncan's fleet. One of the first questions which Nelson put to me, was whether I had been at the Admiralty. I told him there was a rumour that the British fleet had been seen engaged with that of Holland. He started up in his peculiar energetic manner, notwithstanding Lady Nelson's attempts to quiet him, and stretching out his unwounded arm—" Drinkwater," said he, " I would give this other arm to be with Duncan at this moment;" so unconquerable was the spirit of the man, and so intense his eagerness to give every instant of his life to the service of his country.

THE END.

PRINTED BY WILLIAM WILCOCKSON, ROLLS BUILDINGS, FETTER LANE.